Praises for ARIZONA GHOST STORIES by Antonio R. Garcez

"ARIZONA GHOST STORIES gives a hauntingly accurate overview to the many reports of haunted sites all over the state. It not only lists the places from north to south but quotes the interviews of eyewitnesses giving a remarkable feeling of being there with them as they encounter the unknown. Such sites as the Copper Queen Hotel in Bisbee to the Jerome Inn come to life in Mr. Garcez's investigations. His chapter on the reports of ghosts at Tombstone is perhaps one of the best accounts I have seen on this subject."

—Richard Senate

"The accounts range from sweetly sentimental to truly terrifying, but all share the benefit of Antonio's sensitivity and attention to detail. He shows respect for the tales, and those who tell them, and understands that history and culture are inextricably bound to all folklore."

—Jo-Anne Christensen

"Arizona could not have asked for a better chronicler of its supernatural landscape than Antonio R. Garcez. From Arivaca to Yuma, Arizona's most haunted places are all here! These stories will send shivers up your spine, and rightly so—they all really took place! If you ever wanted to experience something paranormal, let this book be your guide!"

—Dennis William Hauck

"These are not long~ago cowboy yarns, hut very real, very current ghost stories from a rich and chilling mix of voices. Antonio has a rare talent for the telling detail; he paints unforgettably creepy images that linger long after the book is done."

—Chris Woodyard

"The reader is transported into the world of the supernatural, by a great storyteller who weaves history and personal interviews into a series of inviting tales, sure to make your skin crawl! Here, restless spirits of the past meet present-day skeptics head on. Memories come to life in the stories from 19 diverse Arizona counties. The thoughtfully told, well researched stories are sometimes frightening, oftentimes chilling, and always fascinating."

—Rob & Anne Wlodarski

Praises for
ADOBE ANGELS GHOST BOOK SERIES OF NEW MEXICO
by Antonio R. Garcez

"This collection of personal encounters with the 'spiritual' or 'supernatural' certainly supported some of my own experiences. These stories are made more frightening by their very proximity."
—*Stephanie Gonzales, NM Secretary of State*

"I highly recommend that both local citizens and visitors to Santa Fe read this book!" —*Sam Pick, Mayor-Santa Fe, NM*

"Fascinating to read, ADOBE ANGELS offers the reader insight into our town's unique traditions, folklore and history; don't miss it!"
—*Frederick A. Peralta, Mayor-Town of Taos*

"Important documentation of the people and history of northern New Mexico. Keep writing!"
—*Kathleen Knoth, Librarian, Millicent Rogers Museum, Taos NM*

"At last someone has written a book about the ghost tales people have been telling here for years!"
—*Tom Sharpe, Albuquerque Journal*

"It's enough to send shivers right up your spine! An excellent effort by Antonio Garcez and I anxiously await his next book!"
—*Dale Kaczmarek, Ghost Research Society*

"GOOD STUFF!" —*Fortean Times Magazine, London, UK*

"If you're a lover of the supernatural, get cozy in an easy chair and prepare your self for the inevitable. Eyewitness accounts told in a straightforward manner!"
—*Tim Palmieri, Western Outlaw-Lawman History Association*

"Another terrifying book from Garcez. I found this one even scarier than the first!"
—*Chris Woodyard, Invisible Ink-Books on Ghosts Hauntings*

"Highly Entertaining!"
—*Mary A. Sarber, Texas Book Columnist, El Paso, Herald-Post*

American Indian Ghost Stories of the Southwest

Antonio R. Garcez

Red Rabbit Press
Truth or Consequences, New Mexico

Other books by Antonio R. Garcez:

Adobe Angels—Arizona Ghost Stories

Adobe Angels—Ghost Stories of O'Keeffe Country

Adobe Angels—The Ghosts of Las Cruces and Southern New Mexico

Adobe Angels—The Ghosts of Santa Fe and Taos

Adobe Angels—The Ghosts of Albuquerque

The author may be contacted for public appearances at the following address:

Red Rabbit Press

P.O. Box 968 • Truth or Consequences, NM 87901

All photos were taken by the author unless otherwise noted.

Cover art by Bonita Barlow

Cover & Book design and typography by

Kathleen Sparkes, White Hart Design

First Edition • Printed in Canada

Library of Congress Catalog Card Number 00-092955

ISBN Number 0-9634029-7-8

Contents

Dedication

To my two American Indian grandparents:

My father's 'Otomi' mother,
Maria Camargo Garcez
Rios, who once told me,
"Never forget that
your umbilical cord is
attached to this land,
so you will always be."

And my mother's
'Mescalero Apache' father,
Juan Ramirez, who sang
and played Apache songs
on his harmonica, to my
young brother and I while
we sat on his lap.

Acknowledgements

My deepest appreciation to the following:

Henry C. Estrada

Thanks to :

Arizona Department of Commerce—
Arivaca Community Profile.

Holbrook Chamber of Commerce/Historical Society of Navajo County (original documents held at Arizona State Archives, Department of Library Archives and Public Records)—Invitations to hanging of George Smiley and Deposition of T.J. McSweeny.

Taos Chamber of Commerce—
City of Taos and Taos Pueblo History

Salinas Pueblo Missions National Monument-
National Park Service—History of the Salinas Pueblo.

Ellen Bigrope, Curator, Mescalero Cultural Center, The Mescalero Apache Tribe-History of the Mescalero Apache.

Betty L. Cornelius, Museum Director-Colorado River Indian Tribes—History of the Colorado Indians.

The Colorado River Indian Tribes, Former Internees of Poston, Veterans and Friends of the Fiftieth Year Observance of the Evacuation and Internment—Historic Content and Memorial Tribute, Poston Arizona.

Author's Note

Some of the names associated with the storytellers mentioned in this book have been changed. This was done for the sole purpose of not identifying those individuals because of their cultural beliefs, or their personal need to disguise their identity. Thus, any name used in the book which might be associated with anyone known to the reader is simply coincidental.

Death is not a period but a comma in the story of life.
I.P. Sculp.

Introduction

This book of ghost stories is the latest in a series of books I've written on ghosts of the Southwest. With this latest project, I've decided to reach specifically into the realm of the American Indian experience with ghosts. The stories contained within these pages, however, are not traditional stories. Almost all of the individuals I interviewed for this book are American Indians who have had first-hand encounters with ghosts. They have seen, and in some cases been spoken to and even physically touched, by spirits. A few of the storytellers, particularly those from New Mexico, are not American Indian, but have an American Indian theme to their stories. I believe the inclusion of Hispanic and Anglo residents imparts a certain interesting quality representative of that state.

The interviews required a considerable amount of editing. As anyone knows who has conducted interviews by transcribing from tape to the written page, the process is not as simple as it might first appear. Careful attention must be paid in order to keep the right "feeling" of the interview. Staying true to the emphasis presented in the interview, keeping the subject matter in context, and attempting to represent in words facial expressions and hand gestures can be challenging, but is not impossible. I attempted to keep the narrative flow and the patois of the person being interviewed as close to genuine as possible, arranging sentences in an orderly manner for the story to proceed smoothly and be understood clearly. While this editing was necessary, it does not detract from the story's principal subject matter. The stories speak for themselves. Undoubtedly, some of them will arouse curiosity, speculation, fear, and even cause a few of you to probe further into the subject of the paranormal. I am content to leave you with more questions than answers. In future books I intend to survey other regions of the United States and compile a collection of similar stories. I have no idea where all this research of eye-witness accounts will lead. Frankly, like you, I am just along for the ride, and thus far it has been a ride of extraordinary wonder and unexpected amazement. Ghost stories engage me. It is simplistic to overemphasize the negative aspects of ghosts as evil or scary. However, focusing on these points alone promotes neither a positive nor hopeful view of our own end result. The best definitions of the existence of ghosts must be viewed through our own personal traditions of cultural and spiritual beliefs. This being said, I am inclined to believe that ghosts do exist and are manifest among us.

American Indian ghost stories that have been past down from their elders reflect a vibrant and diverse array of rich cultural traditions, which in association with unwritten codes of social conduct, have influenced a degree of modern tribal behavior. Examples are in their veneration of sacred sites, prayers, songs, amulets, symbolic dreams, etc. As American Indian society varies from nation to nation, so do their ghost stories. There is no doubt these traditional stories are very important.

American Indians have a strong cultural 'respect' and not "interest" for phenomenon of the spiritual world. It is a world view quite different from western contemporary society. A focus steeped in a not too distant past from which historically, American Indians drew strength, hope, purpose, and visionary direction.

Further, the spiritual cross-over to animal and natural forces is not only acceptable, it was and is today expected. All are valid, all are an integral whole that is vital and fundamental to American Indians.

American Indians had a deep respect for their ancestors. Throughout the centuries before contact with western culture, they used various ways of preparing the bodies of loved ones which in some, but not all cases, were buried underground. Burial was clearly just one of many options available that was utilized. Common funerary rites were cremation, placing the body on a scaffold in the branches of trees, on mountain ledges, in caves, and also being left above ground 'propped-up' in a sitting position against a tree, surrounded by their worldly possessions. And as was the case with pre-colombian nations, entombed within monumental stone pyramids which rivaled those of Egypt.

As I researched this book and spoke to a variety of individuals, I was astonished to discover one recurring principal theme among non-natives. That principal theme was: most every house, barn, retail store, warehouse, etc. which they believe to be haunted, must be, or is, built over an ancient Indian burial ground! How this fixed trend of thought got started eludes me.

What is clear to me, if not to them, is that if this train of thought were true, it stands to reason that the unearthing of native bones and artifacts would be never ending and overwhelming. Indeed, archaeologists would have reported hauntings to such a vast degree that as of today, at least one would have spoken of, or recorded their experience. Clearly there are reports of ghostly activities being manifested about such sites, but not to the considerable degree imagined.

I caution "non-Indians" regarding the use of eagle feathers, sweat lodges, the burning of sage smudge sticks, sweet grass and imitating spiritual, culturally sensitive Native American practices. From Sedona to Santa Fe I've witnessed the exploitative abuse of native culture for the economic gain of labeling one's self "shaman," "medicine healer," etc. Please stop this exploitation! Many centuries of genuine, spiritual Native American leaders with absolute sincerity and knowledge, have utilized the forces of their land and ancestors, for direction and guidance, unlike "self-professed shamans." This process of wisdom is eternal, very personal and self-sacrificing. It is therefore foolish and illogical to assume that non-indians can "instantly" gain such power and status simply by ill-representing themselves to be a "shaman." If non-Native people wish to help Native Americans , a positive first step would be to contact one of the agencies I've listed in the back of this book. Enough said.

Lastly, to all the individuals whom I interviewed for this book, I sincerely thank and wish you all beauty of strength, beauty of patience, beauty of sacrifice, and the internal beauty that ultimately comes with wisdom and humor.

Antonio R. Garcez

Arizona

Yaqui Nation
(Yoeme)

Culturally, the Yaqui or Yoeme nation is descended from the ancient Uto-Azteca, or Mexica people of Old Mexico. In the year 1533, the Spanish made contact with the Yaqui, and ultimately Christianity was introduced, which profoundly altered the Yaqui way of life. Interestingly, the Yaqui embraced Catholicism and the new Spanish system of government, but always kept an independent stance in this union. The Yaqui religious life of today is a result of this merger of ceremonies and cultural beliefs. San Ignacio's Day Fiesta, Easter and Christmas are the most important ceremonies of the year for the modern Yaqui. The Yaqui have a history of being fiercely independent, and resisted Spanish colonialism until 1610, when a treaty was signed between the two. Originally they occupied eight villages in the state of Sonora, Mexico. Due to Mexican political changes, they migrated north to Arizona.

The Yaqui nation was not recognized as an "historic tribe" by the U.S. Bureau of Indian Affairs until 1994. Their battle for such recognition was long and difficult. Considered political refugees because of their migration from Mexico, they were denied the services afforded to other American Indian nations, and thus not recognized as a independent nation and reservation. Presently the population numbers just over 9,000. In Arizona, the Pascua Yaqui Indian Reservation was annexed into the city of Tucson in 1952. The tribal land, 222 acres, was established in 1964 by an Act of Congress and is surrounded by a desert landscape of scenic vistas, drives and trails. The San Ignacio fiesta is observed at Old Pascua, a village located in Tucson that marks the annual fulfillment of the village's obligation to its patron saint, St. Ignatius of Loyola. The Yaqui also currently operate the successful Casino of the Sun. There is another group of Yaqui that reside close to Tempe and Phoenix in the town of Guadalupe. It is from this town that the following story was obtained.

BENJAMIN RED OWL'S STORY

My one and only experience with a ghost took place when I was twenty- six years old, in the summer of 1991. Up to that point, I can't remember ever having had any type of a paranormal experience. Of course there have been times when I've overheard friends and family discuss such things as ghosts and haunted areas, but I've never given the subject much attention. All this changed for me during one summer night in Montana. I had completed four years of graduate work in Art History at the University of Colorado, and with a master's degree under my arm, I made plans to give myself a break from all my hours of study. I thought that rewarding myself with a trip to Canada would be a nice change. Also, I knew that once I entered the job market, it would be a long time before I would have the opportunity to travel for quite some time. In fact, I already had two job offers waiting for me once I returned home. I was in no hurry to return to an office, so I was very eager to begin my trip.

My reason for driving all the way up to Canada was to visit Jerry, a Cree Indian friend, whom I met while attending school. Jerry lived in the province of Alberta, and was a real joker of a guy. Among us Indian students, Jerry was known for his wacky sense of humor. I couldn't wait to get on the road. I packed my small Toyota with all the necessary camping gear—tent and snacks—then got on the interstate heading north to Wyoming, Montana, and my ultimate destination, Canada. Along the way, I spent nights in public campgrounds which were located in state and national parks. Before leaving the northern-most portion of state of Wyoming, I spent six days in the town of Sheridan. Another friend from college, Tom, lived there. Tom is a Lakota Indian who graduated two years before me with a degree in Marketing Management. Tom told me about his friend Joseph who lived in the town of Billings, north of the Crow Indian Reservation. Tom gave Joseph a call and arranged for me to spend a couple of nights at Joseph's house. Joseph was known as a maker of award-winning horse saddles. Tom and I said our good-byes, and off I left to continue my journey north.

I took my time, stopping frequently to take pictures and observing the beautiful prairie landscape. Because of my many sight-seeing stops, I arrived at the Crow Reservation late in the evening. I turned off the highway and found a rest stop where I made camp for the night. In the morning I packed-up my things and drove to the nearest restaurant, got breakfast, then drove to the Little Bighorn Battlefield Monument to have a look. Given its history, and I being Native American, the battlefield was a unsettling place to visit. The Monument's Visitor Center was filled with historical paraphernalia. Being a history buff, I spent a good two hours reading the informational texts, and taking in all descriptions of the artifacts on display. Reading about the major battle that was fought and jointly won by the Sioux and Cheyenne against the invading General Custer was fascinating. I felt proud to be Native American, and at the same time, saddened knowing the present social state that most Indians are locked into. After a few hours, I got in my car and drove on the two-lane road which meandered through the battlefield itself. At one point, I decided to park and go for a hike over the rolling hills and small valleys of the battle site. As I said earlier, I had an uneasy feeling about the place. Standing on the actual ground where the battle was fought many years ago gave me an eerie feeling. I didn't at all feel frightened, just uneasy. After spending several hours hiking about the area, evening was approaching and it began to get dark. I decided to head back to my car, where I had a quick dinner of warm coke, an apple and cookies. Billings was about an hour or two away, so I got back on the highway, anticipating that I'd have a bed at Joseph's house. This plan, as it turned out, was not to be.

After just a few miles on the highway, I noticed that my car was strangely jerking. I knew something was going to give out. Sure enough, just after getting on the interstate, my car altogether stopped. I got out and pushed it to the side of the road. Because I had been told by a mechanic back in Denver that the car's fuel filter needed to be changed, I suspected this was the cause of the problem. I had the foresight to buy a new filter before I left on my trip. Because it was already too dark to get under the hood and replace it, I decided to tackle the problem the next morning. After all, it was not a very long, difficult job to change out the old filter for the new one. Maybe a total of 30 minutes, max. Not far up ahead, I noticed a flat area with tall trees. I decided to push my small car over to this area. I parked the car away from the highway traffic. It seemed like a safe camping site for the night. All the hiking earlier in the day had tired me out. I couldn't wait to get into my sleeping bag and fall asleep. I opened the car's trunk, took out the sleeping bag, and lay it on the ground, with the car creating a buffer between me and the highway. I soon fell asleep.

Sometime during the night, I was awakened by the touch of someone stroking my neck. Because the stroking feeling was not at all sudden or discomforting, at first I was not frightened. Then the thought hit me that someone, a stranger was touching me! I opened my eyes and, still lying in my sleeping bag, I turned around. I gazed in the direction which I imagined a person would be standing. At first I saw nothing in the darkness. Then I saw some movement to my left. My heart was beating hard and I was getting anxious. I turned to look to my left and I saw the image of a small Indian girl. She startled me, and I think I let out a little yell of surprise. I immediately knew this person was a spirit, because her image was vaporlike. She was the same luminous color as the moon, and I could see the trees right through her. I got scared and thought I was going to have a heart attack. I couldn't move. My body was trembling. I don't know why I couldn't find the strength to get up and run. It was if my body was locked with fear. The ghost stood about five feet away from me with a very sad look on her face. She was dressed in a yellow-colored dirty dress, and wore several necklaces made of big beads. She just stood there in front of me staring. I tried to speak, but my voice was weak and my throat was dry. One thing I do remember clearly was the strong scent of wet grass. It was a very earthy scent that I can remember to this day. It's difficult to explain, but I was able to smell and to "feel" the odor of mud, water and grass of a long time ago. It's weird, I know, but that's how I can explain it.

Soon, and with much effort, I managed to get out a yell. She then began to fade away, beginning at her feet and ending at her head. I yelled again, and soon it was all over. She was gone. Sweat was dripping down my face. My ghost encounter took place in what appeared to be all of about five minutes. I got out of the sleeping bag and jumped into the front seat of my car. I locked all the doors, turned on the radio, and after some nervously exhausting minutes pasted, I managed to fall asleep. In the early morning I was awakened when a large noisy semi-truck passed by on the highway. Inside the car, as I moved around, I felt something at the back of my neck. I reached my hand up to scratch, and was surprised when I felt a hardened substance which had attached itself to my hair. I pulled some of this off and looked at my hand. It was hardened mud! I pulled more of this hardened mud off of my neck and head, then I carefully opened the car door, got out and shook the remainder of the dirt from me. I didn't know what to think. Did I have a bad dream during the night, and roll on the ground? Or, did the apparition of the ghost woman rub this mud on me? I didn't care to think anymore about the mud. Frankly, I was eager to repair my car and get the heck out of there!

Now that there was plenty of morning sunlight, I replaced the fuel filter in my car, and after several false starts, got my car going again and hit the highway. Driving north on my way to Billings gave me a few hours to think about what I had experienced the night before. I couldn't believe that I had seen a real ghost just a few hours before. I had lots of questions, with no answers. But the most disturbing question of all was, why did she cover my neck with mud? Was she trying to heal me of an injury? I soon arrived at Joseph's house. Joseph was not home, so I asked his whereabouts at a neighbor's house. After introducing myself to the older woman, she informed me that her neighbor, Joseph Dances Straight, was dead. Apparently, two months prior, while visiting his sister in South Dakota, Joseph and two friends went hunting for deer. One of the shotguns accidently went off, and the blast hit Joseph at the base of his skull, killing him instantly. I was caught off guard by this information. The neighbor was not willing to give me anymore information. I could tell that she and Joseph were close friends. I left her house filled with a numbness. Eventually, I arrived at my friend Jerry's house in Canada. I told him about what I had experienced during my short trip, the ghost woman, and finding out about Joseph's death. Jerry got seriously quiet, then told me that I had been visited by an Indian spirit messenger in the form of a woman. Also, because earlier in the day I had immersed myself in a powerful area—The Little Bighorn Battle Ground—I had "opened myself up" to a spiritual visitor. He went on to say that the messenger had rubbed "medicine" on my neck which symbolized the manner of death which had taken Joseph.

After spending two weeks with Jerry, I returned to my home in Arizona. Never will I forget about my experience with the ghost in Montana. There are lots of things that us Indians need to be aware of. I know that modern society is a very powerful force, but we need to respect and honor our traditions from long ago. These are also very important, and necessary for our people.

Colorado River Indians

The Chemehuevi (Nu Wu)

The Chemihuevi name is derived from a Mohave word that relates to fish. However, the Chemihuevi prefer to distinguish themselves as "Nu Wu" or "people," using their own language when referring to themselves.

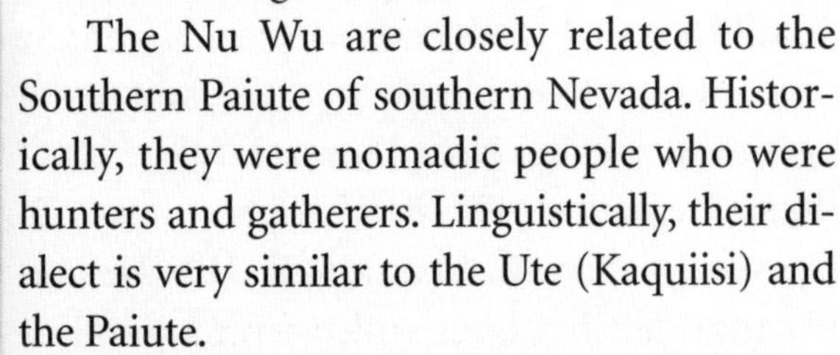

The Nu Wu are closely related to the Southern Paiute of southern Nevada. Historically, they were nomadic people who were hunters and gatherers. Linguistically, their dialect is very similar to the Ute (Kaquiisi) and the Paiute.

Originally, the Nu Wu lived in the area between southern Nevada and Yuma, Arizona, in small family groups. Ancient human habitation is very evident from the numerous petroglyphs (rock carvings), and ancient trails and pictographs (picture writings) that have been discovered in the area. The Colorado River Indian Reservation, created by an act of Congress in 1865, was originally created for just the Nu Wu and Mohave, and was located on their ancestral homeland. But in 1945, the U.S. Government relocated members of the Hopi and Navajo from their traditional lands onto this reservation.

The reservation consists of 278,000 acres of land in the states of Arizona and California. The Colorado River runs directly through the reservation. The almost perfect weather year-round and the rich fertile river-bottom land make farming one of the major industries on the reservation. It is unique in the sense that it is occupied by four distinct tribal groups—Mohave, Nu Wu,

Hopi and Navajo, each with its own separate culture and traditions. As of today, the four tribes that make up the Colorado River Indian Tribes respectively continue to promote and maintain their individual and unique traditional ways, and when necessary, come together and function as one political unit.

Within the reservation is the town of Parker, and next to this is found the Colorado Indian Tribes Museum. The museum displays artifacts, cultural items and artwork of the four nations of Nu Wu, Mohave, Hopi and Navajo. Fame is given to the Nu Wu's highly developed skill of beadwork and basket weaving. Nu Wu baskets are among the finest in the Southwest, and are exquisitely woven using willow, devil's claw and juncus. Sadly, these baskets are becoming more and more difficult to obtain, due to there being fewer weavers who practice the art.

MEMORIAL TRIBUTE:

"To all men and women who honorably served in the United States armed forces in defense of the nation and its people, particularly to those Americans of Japanese ancestry, who, during World War II, fought so valiantly for their country while their parents and families were being interned in the Poston War Relocation Center without due process of law. And to those brave young men who gave their lives in service to their country."

During World War II, the United States was in conflict with Japan. The federal government built several Japanese internment camps on reservations throughout the southwest, purportedly for national security reasons. The Colorado River Tribes area was designated as one of these sites. This historic development brought changes to the reservation. As roads were constructed, land was cleared and innovative agricultural experiments were tested. The results of these experiments successfully raised the economy of the area.

Beginning in May and ending in August 1942, 17,876 Japanese evacuees from the pacific coast states and Arizona arrived to the reservation. Most of the evacuees were from California. The extreme, relentless desert sun scorched the earth, and the frequent winds whipped the sands into blinding dust storms. In winter, chilling winds easily penetrated the walls and wide floor cracks of the flimsily-built tar paper barracks. Adding to the hardships of internment, infrequent but torrential rains would quickly turn the parched dirt walkways and roads into slippery treacherous and muddy quagmires. Amidst the trauma of forced evacuation and the indignities of internment, Japanese children were the first to adapt to the routine of camp life. They found numerous playmates, but they lacked toys and other playthings. Creative parents, relatives and friends relied on their imagination to make playthings from scrap lumber, rocks, trees branches, shells and other available materials for the children.

Betty Cornelius' Story

I'm Nu Wu and I've lived at the reservation most of my life, except for a period of twenty-five years when I got married and lived in Los Angeles, California. Currently I'm the Director of the Colorado Indian Museum and I've held this position for eight years. Before I tell you about the ghostly activity in the area, I need to give a quick historical background of the area, which involved the internment of Japanese Americans at the beginning of World War II. Soon after the bombing of Pearl Harbor, an executive order enacted by then-president Franklin

Delenor Roosevelt stated that, beginning in the city of San Francisco and extending to El Paso, Texas, all Japanese Americans would be placed in several internment camps located throughout the southwest. Our reservation was chosen to be one of these sites.

Another major task was begun by the government at the time of the Japanese relocation. If the government was going to house thousands of people, they would need shelter. Lumber in constructing these houses and barracks would be needed in large quantities. Unfortunately, due to our hot desert climate, such large lumber-producing trees did not grow in the area. The necessary lumber was brought to the reservation by train. It so happened that both the lumber and Japanese were brought to the relocation camp by train. The Japanese were put into boxcars and taken to our reservation. There were in total between eighteen to twenty thousand Japanese who were relocated to three camps in this area, which were named Camp One, Camp Two and Camp Three. The U.S. Government made the Japanese build their own community structures from the lumber that was delivered by these same trains. They built single-family homes and long barracks that were designed to house about ten families. The uniqueness of their architecture was unmistakable. These houses were built in a distinct "pagoda" style. The roof line swung out and curved slightly upward, away from the outside walls, and there was a distinct space between where the roof and the ceiling came together. The Japanese grew vegetables in community gardens, built small ponds, built a movie theatre, and as much as we could tell, they kept up their own cultural traditions. Many babies were born in these camps and many elderly Japanese died at the camps. I heard that some of the dead were taken back to the towns where they were removed from, or shipped back to Japan. I know that several Japanese bodies were buried in the Parker cemetery, just a few miles north of here.

The relocation camps existed for approximately four years,

from 1942 to 1946. When the Japanese were eventually relocated back to the larger society, the houses and barracks which they had built were given to the Colorado Indian Community. The barracks were cut into equal sections of about fifteen to twenty feet wide, by equal lengths long, and distributed to Indian families. A few of these old Japanese houses are still standing on the reservation. Some of these houses which we Indians were given were haunted. Spirits of those Japanese who lived and died within the walls of the houses they built with their own hands refused to move on. I know of one Indian family that moved into one of those Japanese houses, and they had strange things happen. Doors of the house would open and close on their own. A chair would move away from the table as if pushed by invisible pair of hands. As if someone was about to seat themselves down for a meal, the chair would move away from the table, then it would move back against the table! Also, lights would go on and off at all hours. Other times, many times, Indian families talked about seeing the shadowy, ghostly outline of a person who walked in their houses, from one room to the next. At times these ghosts would walk through a room, approach the front door and then pass through it and go outside.

Other common reports are about the sound of ghostly footsteps on the wooden floors of these old houses at all hours of the day and night. Families would even hear the sound of rattling dishes in their kitchens, as if the ghosts were going through the daily task of washing dishes after a meal. Some families reported hearing very young babies crying. I know that the people were concerned about these ghosts, but for whatever reason, eventually they got accustomed to their "visitors." They knew why the ghosts were occupying their houses, and about the Japanese sad history, so Indian families knew they would not be hurt by the ghosts. They just decided to live with them. Some families "smudged" their homes with sage smoke and offered prayers to the spirits. Not too long ago, a group of traditional Japanese people visited our reservation and performed religious ceremonies. It was sad to see because they would break down and cry and hug each other. There is so much sorrow and sadness associated with the relocation. The Japanese built a stone monument on our reservation to mark that part of their history.

Being a Nu Wu, I've been very accustomed to seeing things that non-Indians would regard as supernatural. I know that these things do exist so I have been raised to be very respectful and just to let them be. I can sense the presence of shadows and light, or auras that animals have. It's something that comes natural to me. Many of our Native American people still practice our beautiful religion. I also know that there are "spiritual power sites" in the hills and mountains located in the reservation and in the surrounding area. There is a lot of very powerful energy here. I know that our medicine people know about these sacred areas and spiritual sites, but we don't talk about these places to anyone. That's just the way it is.

Franklin McCabe III's Story

I'm a Navajo and originally from Provo, Utah. I'm currently employed at the reservation as the Recreation Director of our gymnasium, Irataba Hall. I've lived at this reservation for twenty-two years, since I was three years old. My first experience with a ghost took place when I was approximately five years old. I recall that I was lying on my bed in my room, day dreaming about something. Suddenly, I heard something moving. I turned my head in the direction of where there was a rocking chair. Then I saw the strangest thing—the chair was rocking back and forth all on its own! There was

no wind coming into the room from my window and, at the time, I was all alone in the house. It just kept rocking and rocking. Then it stopped. I did tell my parents about this, but perhaps because I was a child, they must have thought it would be best to say nothing. But sometime later, when she thought I was old enough to know and after we had moved out of the house, my mother told me that a woman used to live in our house prior to us, and the woman's bedroom, where she had died, was my bedroom. Of course when I heard this, I was startled by the news, and reflected on all the time I had spent in that room by myself. As I said before, the rocking chair was my first experience with something ghostly. But as recently as two years ago, I had a more direct and scary encounter. An ongoing haunting, which is kind of common knowledge on the reservation, takes place at the gymnasium which I manage. Our gymnasium has quite an interesting history. Prior to 1965, there was a hospital located on the grounds, utilizing a portion of the gymnasium. I understand that the Japanese who were held in the nearby interment camps during the war were sent to this hospital. I don't think people would disagree with me about the fact that perhaps the hauntings at the gym have something to do with this history. A lot of people on the reservation have heard the stories about the gymnasium being haunted, and some can even give their own stories about seeing apparitions or ghosts there.

Beginning at the start of my employment at the gymnasium, I and others have many times felt the presence of a heaviness, or a sense of negativity, there. My experience at the gymnasium began one evening as I arrived to finish some work I had started earlier in the day. I and two friends arrived at around about 5 p.m. Having the only keys, I unlocked the front entrance door, and we all made our way into the kitchen. We were planning a barbecue the following day, so we were there to check on the supply of food for the event. We were alone in the building, just the three of us. As we went about our business, we were startled by the sound of a very high-pitched woman's scream coming

from the basketball court. The scream was so eerie that it sent chills up all our spines. We looked at each other and immediately high-tailed it out of the gymnasium to the parking lot where we had parked our car. I guess reason must have stepped in and made me think that perhaps the scream was caused by a woman in trouble. We talked among ourselves and decided to cautiously return to the gym and search for an injured woman. As we re-entered the building we kept our ears and eyes ready for any suspicious noise or movement. We searched the whole gymnasium, looking in lockers and under the bleachers. All the doors were locked and the bathrooms and halls were empty. We found no evidence of anyone being inside.

Not long after this, there was another haunting incident that occurred one evening, during a youth sleep-over at the gymnasium. The kids brought their sleeping bags and everyone gathered on the stage area of the basketball court. The plan that night was to sleep on the stage floor. Once all the kids were inside the gym, I closed and locked all the doors, making sure there were no drugs or alcohol that might be sneaked into the facility. As the evening progressed, I was having a conversation with a student, while everyone was talking and having their own lively social interactions. I was standing, facing the student, having a clear and direct view of the two doors that open to the hallway out from the basketball court. Then something unusual caught my eye. I noticed a white ghostly figure which was standing at one of the doors! It also must have noticed me looking in its direction, because it moved away into the hall. Startled, I kept still. Then it quickly reappeared at the next door! I can explain the image as being a big white blur-like vapor. Apparently, I was not the only one at the time who witnessed the apparition, because when I mentioned what I had just seen to those gathered next to me, a few students excitedly admitted they also saw the exact same ghostly figure. This apparition left us un-nerved to the extent that we all agreed to gather together in the middle of the basketball court and sleep close to each other in a big circle. Our sense of safety in numbers soon came to a sudden end. As we were about to call it a night, every single storage door located below the stage where we had been gathered just a few minutes before swung open. Seeing this, everyone got quite scared. I had to explain to everyone that there was nothing to be afraid of, and with some effort, eventually emotions settled down.

Another paranormal experience took place at the gymnasium during, of all times, a 1998 Halloween event. Once again, several persons were there to serve as witnesses. At the time, the gymnasium was decorated with halloween paper decorations, and everyone was in the mood for a good time. The event was entitled: "The Haunted Gym." It wasn't long before our festive attitude ended. Hours before the evening's festivities were to begin I, along with my assistants, made sure that no was was in the gym aside from us and a couple of helpers. We were all gathered in the basketball court discussing something or other, when the sound of footsteps began. We immediately got quiet, and the sound of someone moving paper started up. We knew that the ghosts were walking about once again. Knowing the stories of the gymnasium being haunted, we decided to exit the gym, and wasted no time in running out the door! Once outside, a few of us with a bit more bravery decided to re-enter the gym and investigate. My younger 15-year-old brother accompanied me with four other helpers, as we did a security walk-through. Once more we heard the footsteps start up, only this time they were just about six feet away from us! What a scare! We stood looking at each other with big, wide eyes. We soon joined the others waiting for us outside.

There have also been instances when objects at the gymnasium were be moved by invisible hands. I know that there have been some faculty who have seen basketballs bounce without being touched. The former director of the gym is one person who tells of watching a basketball, at rest on the floor, start to slowly move, then begin to bounce on its own across the floor! I was alone at the gym one night and witnessed a ball which came rolling toward me, then passed behind me. There was no way that this ball could have been pushed. I was alone at the gymnasium. The floor is level and the ball was stationary. We have begun a series of upgrades at the gym, such as applying new paint and other such renovations, attempting to make the facility a more inviting and friendly place for the public to visit. I know there are many who do not want to enter the building, but hopefully things will change. My goal is to have medicine men bless and rededicate the gym to the community by July 1, 2000.

Another ghostly experience took place just three years ago at my house. One night, while getting over an illness, I was lying in bed and happened to look out my bedroom door at the hallway. Suddenly, I felt a very heavy presence in the room. At the same time I also heard the sound of a loud hum. I'm not sure what this sound was, but it was followed by another strange thing. The atmosphere in my bedroom felt to me as if it was becoming thick. This was followed by a strong mass of weight that began to push me down against the bed. The force was so strong and heavy against my chest that it made my breathing stop. I began to panic. Then I saw a figure appear slowly at my doorway. It moved its arms back and forth, and then it paused and looked in my direction. The ghost had the outline of a man, and it was very dark, like a shadow. With all my might, I tried to break away from the hold that this force had taken over me. With much effort, I extended one arm and tried to yell, but I could not make a sound. The dark shadow just stood at the door and stared at me. Then it moved away with a bouncing, walking motion. At the same time, the heavy weight lifted off me and I began to breathe normally.

About six months after this incident, I was awakened by our dogs barking outside my bedroom. I got out of bed and walked to the window to have a look. In our backyard we have a motion sensitive security light on a pole. The security light turned on as I got to the window. As I pulled up the shade and peered outside to have a look, there in the window staring back at me was the same dark, shadowy figure that I had seen before in my doorway! It was just a few inches from my own face, on the other side of the window! I was terrified! I automatically let go of the shade cord, and it quickly unrolled and hit the window sill with a bang! I got into bed and shook with fright. I kept repeating to myself, "Oh God, oh God." Eventually I fell asleep.

In 1996, I, my mother and my brother had another ghost experience at about 10 p.m. That night we heard someone pound hard on our window, while an excited male voice in distress yelled out, "Natani, Natani!" Natani is my brother's name, so we quickly ran to the window and then outside. We saw no one. The dogs didn't even bark. We grabbed our guns and looked everywhere and found nothing. We all assumed that it was a spirit voice attempting to contact us for some unknown reason. Many times in our kitchen we've experienced our microwave oven, lights, and refrigerator go on and off. This only happened in the kitchen. Now this might sound as if we had problems with our electrical wiring, but I know that this was not the case. My parents decided to have our local Mormon elders pay us a visit and conduct a prayer service to get rid of the negative presences. Prior to the service, the elders instructed my family to keep our eyes closed and not to speak, and to keep our minds clear. We all sat in a circle in the living room and as the service began, a low moaning sound started up in the kitchen, like a dog howling at the moon. As the service continued, the moaning sound became louder and louder. At one point, with my eyes still closed, I felt as if the whole house was rocking me back and forth, and I felt a powerful gust of wind that was moving in and out of the space between me and the others. Then I felt something begin to brush me on my left, then whatever it was started to moved over to my right side. This "thing" brushed up and down against my arms. I kept my eyes closed tightly. Then the moaning sound became clear to me as it got louder and louder. It was the word "No"! Imagine, if you can, the word "no" being stretched out in a loud, long, "Noooooooo!" That's how it sounded. Then suddenly the noise was gone. About a minute passed and although we were instructed not to open our eyes, or say a word, I slowly opened my eyes. I decided to break the tension and silence by saying, "Did you guys hear that?" As soon as I finished saying these words, everyone opened up and began to say,"Yeah, I heard it, did you, yeah, etc." Then the elders got up, said a quick good-bye and were out the door! We got a "kick" out of their reaction. As of this day, that was the last incident of any ghostly activity that I have experienced.

MARICOPA AK-CHIN

The Maricopa nation's history is one of constant battles with neighboring tribes. Their numbers were small and they claimed their homeland as being along the lower Gila and Colorado rivers. In 1825, a major event took place when their friendly neighbors, the Pima, welcomed the Maricopa into their villages. This union obviously benefited the Maricopa, as now aggressive attackers had a much larger, united force to confront. In the year 1864, settlements of Mormons from the northern state of Utah had begun in the area, but not unnoticed by the watchful eyes of the Apaches. The Apaches loathed the intrusion of their land by these alien strangers and attacked the settlements with gusto. The Mormons obtained the help of both the Pima and Maricopa who acted as scouts and security. This focal area was in Lehi, which today the Maricopa retain as part of the reservation. Maricopa red-clay, geometrical pottery is now sought by collectors for its beauty and creative use of shape. Like the Pima, they have prospered in modern society.

ALBERT JOAQUIN MANUEL SR.

I'm Maricopa and I've lived in this area all my life. I'm fifty-eight years old. As a kid I would see many things in my dreams. Visions, lots of things. I worked as a farm worker some years ago, in the small town of Standfield, just a few miles away. I remember the times, when I was working some nights, several fellow workers would talk among themselves about seeing what we called, "El Cu-cui," or the boogieman, in the fields. The workers would speak about seeing ghost lights and other strange things.

There were nights when they would get so scared that they would leave work and go home. But I wasn't scared, and everyone knew this. So my boss would send me to where this ghost was seen to finish the job on the farm. I never actually saw El Cu-cui, but I did hear it. Back in 1958 when a lot of us Indians were in the fields picking cotton, there were some guys who died out in the fields. They were young Indians who committed suicide. I never found out why. I guess they were depressed or something. Not long after their deaths, we would all hear and experience very scary things. At the time, all the farm workers slept together in a common room, and at night when the lights were turned off, strange noises would start-up and our beds would start to shake. I remember even being touched all over my body while lying in bed. My face would be touched and my arms would be held tightly by invisible hands. I knew this was caused by the deaths of the guys who died in the fields. It was their spirits. I remember also smelling a cologne or perfume in the room.

That same year, there was one Indian man who was killed one night, after leaving a bar. While at the bar he got into a fight with another guy. After the fight, he left the bar and walked home. As he was walking along the road, the guy he had the fight with came looking for him in his car. When the driver spotted him walking on the side of the road, he drove his car over him and killed him. The hit-and-run took place right next to a big tree, not far from here.

The next day some Indians dug a quick hole and buried the man's body. The hole must not have been very deep because the coyotes soon smelled the body, and dug some of it up. I remember walking by the shallow grave and seeing the dead man's leg and foot bones sticking out of the dirt. I didn't see his head, just the leg bones. A few days later, whenever local residents would

"The hit-and-run took place right next to a big tree, not far from here."

walk by the shallow grave, they would make sure to carry some rocks with them. They dropped these rocks on top of the grave to prevent the coyotes from digging up more of the body. Eventually someone removed the body, and took it to our cemetery for reburial.

I also recall, about ten years ago, when a deadly cabin fire took the life of a baby. It must have been a very hot fire because there was nothing left of the cabin but ashes. It was located next to a big field that I used to work in. Well, one night not long after that fire, as I was irrigating the field, I clearly heard the cries of the baby that died in that fire. The cries lasted for about seven minutes. I wasn't scared, but soon after I heard the baby crying, a pack of coyotes surrounded me. I decided get away from the coyotes. As I began to leave the field, one coyote who must have been the leader, came forward and followed me as I walked away. At the time I was carrying a gun, so I raised the gun, showing it to the coyote. When it saw the gun, it back away.

As a child, I grew up knowing the stories of "messengers" that take the form of owls. These owls roost high in the trees. They hoot to get the attention of a person passing by. I was told that this sign is a message to the person, to let them know that something is soon going to happen to them. A death will take place, of a cousin or someone close to the person. Whenever I see these owls, I chase them away. I throw rocks at them until they fly off.

There were also times when I would see figures of people walking down the road and I would hear people talking behind trees. Even though I could see that there was no one behind the trees, I could hear their voices speaking to one another. All of this never scared me. Recently in our kitchen we have experienced strange things. In the evening, as soon as my wife and I go to bed, noises will start. We hear footsteps walking slowly in the living room and then in the kitchen. The ghosts will turn the water facets on and off, and we can hear the salt shakers being moved about the table. It's a real loud noise that the ghost makes. These ghosts seem to always be around. I guess they want to do what they did while they were alive. But like I said, I'm not scared.

WHITE MOUNTAIN APACHE

(Nde, Indeh or Tinneh)

The White Mountain Apache have the notable history of being the direct descendants of the original Apache tribes who settled the area many centuries ago. The ancestral homeland of the White Mountain Apache Nation is located in the east central region of Arizona. The Apache are now a nation comprised of several independent bands throughout the Southwest.

The reservation encompasses 1.6 million acres. It was established by Executive Order on November 9, 1891. Strongly traditional in culture and spirituality, the nation currently has over 12,000 members. Historically, they were hunters and raiders who did some farming, but in many cases carried out raids on neighboring agricultural-based villages for food that they were unable to obtain by hunting. The Apache consider the mountains that surround their lands to be holy and the source of their spirituality. The Spaniards, Anglos and Mexicans were unsuccessful in their numerous attempts to subdue these true guerrilla warriors. As with almost everything ever written about the Apache, it is important for the reader to question the source of the written word, due in large part to a negatively-skewed view regarding the Apache being linked to vast amounts of atrocities. In fact, this cautious approach should be taken when reading most anything printed about Native People—period.

Today a wide range of accommodations that include dining,

shopping and gaming at the Hon-Dah Casino are available on the reservation.

Catherine Two Bear's Story

In 1992, I was attending the University of Arizona in Phoenix. I was in my senior year and majoring in biology. During the summer of that same year, five seniors (including myself), four graduate students and a professor were conducting field work at Theodore Roosevelt Lake. The Lake is located in the Tonto National forest, about a two-hour drive northeast of Phoenix. Our two-month study and research focused on native amphibians of the lake, specifically bullfrogs. Throughout the years, this particular species of frog had begun to change the ecology of Arizona's lake and streams. Although the bullfrogs had increased in populations, other smaller native population of frogs were showing the beginning signs of extinction. Bullfrogs have a voracious appetite and will consume anything smaller than themselves, including snakes, other frogs, lizards and mice. Our focus of study was to specifically record data, and ultimately discover a link to the bullfrog population explosion.

Although I enjoyed the research field work, it was wet, muddy, smelly and I had to wade in waist-deep cold water. In order to catch the frogs, I had to dress in water-tight rubber overalls. Also part of my uniform was a net laundry bag which I tied to my belt, a pith helmet with a flashlight strapped on top, and of course a fish net attached to a four foot pole. I and my colleagues would get in the water at about eight in the evening and begin our "hunt," which would last until around ten or so at night. We initiated a process of surprise by which we would catch these fast and alert bullfrogs by slowly wading towards a floating mass of leaves or plants. Using the light strapped to my helmet, I would scan the area until I spotted the bright tell-tale sign of a bullfrog's reflecting eyes. Once spotted, I would make my way towards the frog, careful not to make any ripples and, using my fishing net, quickly catch it and place it inside the net bag tied to my belt.

This system, although primitive, would bring in about ten to twenty frogs a night per student. Each pair of students had a section of lake in which to capture the frogs. After finishing our work for the night, we would drive back to the lab and place the frogs in a large stock-water tank for study the next day. Our evening captures took place three nights a week. Due to the many frogs in the area, we had enough specimens and paperwork to keep us very busy.

So what does capturing bullfrogs have to do with ghosts? Well, one evening during a night of bullfrog catching, something very, very strange happened to me. Another girl and I went off for the evening to do the night's frog-gathering. We went into the water at about eight in the evening. The frogs were making their croaking sounds as usual, and we got right to work. But at about nine o'clock, I began to feel sick. My stomach was turning. I figured it was something I had eaten earlier at dinner. I decided to end the evenings hunt and get back to my warm bed. I informed my partner that I would be taking the truck, and for her to catch a return ride to the lab with the others. "No problem," she said. So off I drove. The road was dark. I had to drive slowly due to javalinas (wild desert pigs) and other small animals that were out and about. It was summer, so to get fresh air, I had both the windows in the truck lowered. Suddenly, I felt something come in through the passenger side window! Something hit the right side of my body and gave me a terrible scare! I quickly put on the brakes and nervously turned on the interior truck light. Then I saw it—a small owl! Apparently the owl had flown across my path on the road, and mistakenly entered the truck through the open window. Well, there it was, on the floor of the truck flapping its wings with its beak wide open. I can look back now and say, that confused bird gave me a good scare! I opened my drivers' side door and scrambled outside. I walked over to the passenger side door and opened it, to allow the owl a way out. But when I opened the door the owl was gone! Where had it gone? I carefully looked under and behind the truck seat, but there was no owl. If it had exited the truck on its own,

I would have heard it, or even seen it because the light was still on inside the truck. This was definitely a strange thing that had just occurred. The owl in my truck simply disappeared! Knowing something about animal behavior, I knew that this was not usual. Also, being an Apache gave me a cultural knowledge about such things. Traditional Apache people do not consider owls to be positive animals to be associated with. I knew this owl was not a good omen. Owls to Apaches are messengers of bad news, and even death. My parents have told me that some medicine people who do evil use the owl's spirit in their witchcraft.

I quickly got back into the truck, rolled up both windows and drove at a fast speed to the cabin. I admit that at the time, I was scared being all by myself. When I entered the cabin, I went straight to the bathroom and showered. I still had the stomach ache, but now I was more concerned about my recent owl incident. After making sure that all the doors in the cabin were locked, and the outside light was on, I got into bed and waited for the return of the others. After about twenty minutes, no one had returned, and I began to get worried. I got out of bed and looked out the window, and saw nothing but darkness. I thought it best to try and sleep, even though my stomach was a ball of nerves. As soon as I got back into bed, I heard the sound of footsteps in the front room. I knew there was no way someone could have entered the cabin without opening the locked door and making a sound. Something bad was definitely going on, and I was scared! As I gazed from my bed at the open doorway that led into the bedroom, the footsteps stopped. Then there was silence for a few seconds. Soon I heard the voice of what sounded like a small child say in my Apache language, "Can I go see mama, I want to see Mama, can I go see mama?" I couldn't stop trembling. The words were very clear, and because they were spoken in Apache, that made them even more terrifying to me.

I had had enough of this, so I jumped out of the bed and, in the darkness, scrambled for the light switch on the wall. Nervously, I tripped over my own shoes, fell to the floor hitting my left shoulder, and smashed my big toe against the dresser. I was in pain. I figured my toe was broken. I managed to crawl across the floor, then find the wall with the light switch, turn it on, and crawl to the bathroom.

No sooner had I entered the bathroom, I heard the sound of my fellow students' trucks returning to the lab. I was an emotional mess. I decided it would be best not to tell anyone about what had happened to me. After all, what could they say or offer me? One thing that I did need was to get some medical help for my toe. It was already swelling up when my roommate came in the door. I told her that I had fallen, and that was all. I was driven that night to the student university clinic in Phoenix, where an x-ray was taken, and I was given the good news that the toe was not broken. Still it hurt quite a lot and was very bruised. Unable to do any more night wading for frogs in cold lake water, my research ended. I spent the remainder of the summer at home. Once I arrived home, I told my parents all about the experience with the owl, and the child's ghostly voice. They told me to pray and to never again be out alone in that area. My parents could not offer an explanation regarding the owl that came into my truck, or the ghostly voice of the child. All I was told was that sometimes these "things" are forces that foretell a future event. As of this date, I have not had anything happen to me that I can connect to that summer night in 1992. But, that does not mean I won't. I'm hoping not to ever experience anything like that again. I'm not the type of person that goes looking for ghosts and things. Ghosts scare me.

San Carlos Apache

The San Carlos Apache Indian Reservation is located east of Phoenix in southeastern Arizona and was established by Executive Order on November 9, 1871. The total land mass of the reservation is just under 1,900,00 acres. The reservation was reduced in size a total of five times for the benefit of copper and silver miners and eager Mormons whose demand for water surrounding the Gila Valley reduced it further. It is the seventh largest U.S. reservation, with over 7,100 people. Within the reservation borders are forested alpine meadows and wooded mountains, as well as desert plains. Anthropologists speculate that the Apache nation entered this region around 1450. The San Carlos Apache call themselves "t'iis ebah nnee" or "grey cottonwood people" and their language is closely related to the Di-neh' (Navajo). The San Carlos Apache now consider themselves to be a unified people, even though their history shows they were originally several separate bands of the same Native nation.

After his surrender in 1873, the great Apache chief Cochise, along with his followers was forcibly taken by the U.S. military to San Carlos. Soon after, the famous medicine man Geronimo and his followers fled the oppression of the San Carlos Reservation. Presently, the reservation fights the continuous battle of arduous unemployment among its people, with the hope of further developing industry and tourism. Encouragingly, tourism is taking hold as a source of income and employment. The tribe is directly promoting its lakes and forests, focusing on campers and sportspeople. The cattle-ranching industry and the mining of Peridot, a semiprecious stone found within the reservation, is also a source of employment. The largest nearby town of Globe provides needed medical and shopping facilities.

HENRY TALL HORSE'S STORY

My mother died when I was two years old, and since that time, I've lived in San Carlos with my father. My experience was with two spirits. Everyone seems to think that ghosts only appear during the night, but in my case, I saw them during the day. These spirits didn't harm me, but I still got pretty scared. My experience was a strange and powerful one that I know will stay with me for a long time.

One spring morning, when I was nineteen years old, a close friend and I decided to walk over to the nearby San Carlos river and fish for catfish. Before heading out, we found two metal beer can openers. We used two stones to pound them flat, and made them into spear points. We sharpened the metal points, grinding them against a large flat boulder. Then we wrapped each of these points with wire to the ends of long thin, but strong, poles. It was a primitive but effective tool in spearing fish. My friend and I went fishing like this many times before, so we were eager to catch a lot of fish. It was about 10 a.m. when we got to the river. We followed the river bed until we found a spot with a few trees to shade us from the sun, and a pool of water that we hoped had some fish. We each sat on the sand at opposite sides of the pool. Because the pool of water was a short distance from the main river, the water was still. In this still water, it was easy to spot the movement of swimming fish. We fished for a few hours, and caught five fish. We decided to head home and fry the fish for lunch. Most Apache I know don't like to eat fish because of our traditional beliefs, but that is changing. My friend and I enjoy eating fish. After our catfish lunch, my friend went home to his house and I took a nap.

Around 6 p.m. I decided to walk back to the river, only this time I just wanted to walk and not fish. I followed the path back to the pool of water where my friend and I had been earlier. As I got closer, in the distance I heard a very strange sound. The sound was a humming or buzzing noise that I couldn't identify. I decided to investigate by following the sounds up the river bed ahead of me. The sun was starting to go down in the west, but there was still plenty of light. As I got closer, the noise seemed to change to something like the flapping wings of a large flock of birds. I decided to slow my pace in order not to surprise whatever might be making the noise. I walked as carefully as I could through the trees and spiny weeds. I had a feeling that animals might be nearby, so when I thought I was close enough, I stopped and got behind a large tree branch to hide myself. Flies were buzzing around my head, but I didn't want to make any noise by swatting them. I got down on my stomach and lay flat on the sand, so I wouldn't be seen. In the distance, not far from me, I could see two large shadow-like figures. They were about 70 yards away from me and I was unable to make out what they were. At first I thought they were two large dogs. They were about the same size as german shepherds. I strained my eyes to see the figures. Suddenly they changed into a shape that looked like a human figures! They were definitely not dogs, and I knew they were definitely not human either! As I said before, there was plenty of sunlight, so darkness was not a problem. Also, something like cloth, or maybe even animal skins, hung loose over their bodies. I couldn't tell what this stuff was. The figures had arms and legs, hands and feet, and their faces were covered with this cloth like stuff. This covering made it impossible to a make out their faces. I saw them bent over on their hands and feet, walking just like a four legged animal.

While I was watching all this take place, coming from the direction of the figures was the flapping wing noise that I had heard earlier. There were no birds anywhere and no wind blowing either! But I could hear the noise of what sounded to me like a tremendous flock of birds' wings flapping! These mysterious figures stood up, bowed down, turned around, and slowly moved away from each other. Several times they got down on all fours, and for many minutes, turned in complete circles. It seemed like they were dancing. Something inside told me that these "things" were not normal, but in fact "spirits." I was scared. I tried my best to keep very still, but I was shaking all over. After a few minutes, the spirits changed their steps and began to move from side to side. I know this might sound crazy, but the figures changed from animal to human to animal and back again. I couldn't believe what I was seeing! Suddenly, they did something that scared me even more: they stood upright on their feet, and leaped towards each other. I'm telling you, this really surprised me. I didn't expect them to do this, or to be so fast. I felt that if I moved, even a finger, they would discover me. Who knows what they would have done to me. Because they were moving all around the riverbed so much, I was afraid they would eventually spot me. I decided to keep lying flat on my stomach, hoping to camouflage myself as much as possible. If they spotted me, I was ready to run for it. I kept quiet and watched them repeat their strange dance over and over again. A few times one of them would jump about ten feet into the air. It was terrifying and, at the same time, fascinating to watch.

I stayed hidden behind the branch for a few more minutes, until I felt a bug sting my leg. I felt it crawl into my pant leg and sting me on the ankle. It must have been a wasp because it hurt like heck! I didn't want to make a sudden move, but knew I needed to get rid of it. I slowly sat up and stretched my arm over to scratch my leg. Through it all, I didn't take my focus off the spirits. Luckily, they didn't notice me. But when I turned my head, I hit it against a branch that was a few inches above me. The sound of the moving branch gave me away! I saw the spirits freeze and immediately they turned their heads in my direction! I saw them crouch down and instantly disappear into thin air! That was all I needed. I stood up and ran for my life, breaking branches as I ran through the bushes. Several times I lost my balance and fell to the ground. Each time I got up and ran back down the river retracing my steps, stumbling many more times before arriving at the road which led back home. It's difficult for me to describe how scared I was. I was shaking all over.

When I got home, my father saw me covered in sweat and dirt and asked me where I had been. I excitedly told him the story of what I had seen. He looked at me with a strange gaze that I had never seen before and shook his head. He said, "Those were not things you should have been watching. You should not have been sneaking up on those spirits. They need to be left alone when they dance. You must not ever sneak up on spirits again." He also told me: "The spirits come down from the mountains from time to time." They have been doing this since Apaches first came to this area. The spirits live in the mountains and canyons. They follow the water because there is power in water. The river is like a big vein and water is the blood of life for spiritual beings. You need to go back there to where you saw the spirits, and leave them an offering." I told my father that I would do as he said, but as of this day, I have not gone back to that spot. I don't want to see any more spirits. Knowing that the spirits did not wish to cause me any harm has changed my view of spiritual things, but I'm still not wanting to meet any more of them. I was raised with the stories of spirits that lived in the nearby mountains around our reservation, and was told of witches and ghosts that took many animal forms. Years ago it took my own personal experience with the dancing spirits to prove to me that these were not just stories. I know these spirits are real because I have seen them.

HUALAPAI

In times past, beginning around 600, the Hualapai were a tribe who were primarily hunter-gatherers. But where water was available, the Hualapai cultivated gardens of corn, squash and beans. Today there are just under 2,000 Hualapai who live at the tribal headquarters in Peach Springs, Arizona, 50 miles east of Kingman on Historic Route 66. The total reservation encompasses 108 miles of the Colorado River and a segment of the Grand Canyon. The topography of the reservation varies from rolling grassland and shear, rugged canyons to pine forest. Elevations range from 1,500 feet at the Colorado River's banks to over 7,300 feet at Aubrey Cliffs. The Hualapai nation has managed to maintain their culture, language and well-deserved pride. The future looks positive for the Hualapai, especially since they currently have one of the highest number of students who are enrolled in college of any reservation in the state.

ROBERT RED SKY'S STORY

One winter in the month of January, when I was seventeen, my brother and father, along with my father's two good buddies, went on a deer-hunting trip in the Hualapai valley. This was a hunting trip that none of us will ever forget. Even now a strange feeling comes over me when I think back to what we all witnessed years ago, on what started out to be just an ordinary outing. That winter day I experienced an example of the power of spirits that come forth from the land the Hualapais call home.

Two weeks before, my father had spoken to three Indian fellas in town. These guys mentioned to him about the big deer bucks they had seen browsing and running within a deep canyon. To offer further proof, they asked my father to walk with them out to the road where their pick-up truck was parked. The men proudly pulled off a large plastic tarp which was covering the bucks they had killed. He told me those guys had some of the most beautiful bucks he had ever seen. He asked the three guys for detailed directions regarding the location of their successful hunting. As they gave him directions, he wrote down every road, turn and curve. In our Indian way, we don't hold back information about such hunting areas. It's traditionally right that we share such information among our people, and it's something that goes back a long way with the Hualapai.

My father arrived home and told my brother and I about the deer. Soon we had planned a hunting trip. My father was convinced he too could shoot a deer or two just like those guys in town had. He got on the phone and invited two good friends of his. The date was set.

We knew the weather would be cold so we packed a good supply of food and warm clothes. My father enjoys eating hot chile so my mom made him about two dozen beef burritos with some very hot red chile, all rolled up in foil. These he planned to heat up on the camp fire. We loaded the pick-up with three days supply of food and water, the burritos and our hunting gear, then off we drove to meet up with my father's two friends.

We started out in the early morning, and although it was a very cold winter morning, there was no snow on the ground. The weather was perfect. We soon came to the main turn-off from the highway. It was a dirt road which was not too rough for the first five miles but

"We soon came to the main turn-off from the highway."

"We followed an old coyote trail that went down the eastern side of a ridge."

then got very rough as we made another turn on to another road. The sun was already up in the east as we started our way up over a hill. We stopped at the top of the hill and took a short coffee break. As we stood standing around the two trucks in the empty landscape drinking our hot coffee, we suddenly heard a strange sound come from the west. It was like the sound of a hundred hoofbeats, the sound of many horses going at a full gallop. It came from nowhere; it just sort of started up and lasted for a few seconds, then it ended. We expected to see a herd of horses come up onto the hill, but there was nothing visible, not even a dust cloud. None of us could explain what it was. We nervously joked about it being a flying jet, but the sky was, as far as we could see, clear of any aircraft. Not saying another word, we finished our coffee, got back into the trucks and continued on our way.

The time now was eight-thirty in the morning and I could tell that the trucks were not going to be able to continue any further on the very rocky road we were driving on. We decided to stop and make camp in the middle of a distant, small grove of juniper trees. The wind was still and the air was cold and crisp as we opened our tents and arranged them around a rock fire ring that my brother formed. After making camp we decided to eat some food, and then head out with our rifles towards the hills in the direction we were told the deer would be. We followed an old coyote trail that went down the eastern side of a ridge. We were careful not to talk loudly, or make loud sounds with our footsteps. Deer are very alert and can be easily spooked. We noticed that the area was littered with deer droppings. A good sign! The area was sparsely spotted with medium to tall junipers, and in the distant narrow valleys were a few groves of cottonwoods and oaks. My father knew that deer like to browse in these areas, so we were constantly trying to pick out any movement in the distance. Suddenly, just as earlier before, the weird sound of hoofbeats started up again. We all stood still and waited. Then, just as before, the sound came toward us and soon disappeared. This time we were not so quick to dismiss the sound as being a jet plane. We softly spoke among ourselves, but said nothing about it being an omen of bad medicine. We knew it would not be a good thing to talk about it any further, because to do so would bring us a bad hunt.

We again picked up the hike and continued towards the valley below. The time was now one in the afternoon, three hours since we left our camp site. As we entered the valley and the grove of tall trees, we were startled as a porcupine came out from behind an old stump and gave us all a fright. It was difficult to keep from laughing loudly. We all felt a sense of relief at our little friend's sudden appearance. As we exited the other side of the grove of trees, my father, who was now walking ahead of us, spotted some deer on the side of the hill. He stopped his walk and lowered his left hand, exposing the palm, which was a signal for us all to immediately stop. We stood still and viewed the deer, quietly scanning the large herd before us. There were ten does and three really beautiful bucks. What a sight! This was what we had all dreamed of. We spoke in soft voices, communicating to each other how best to get a shot at the bucks. Then, without warning, something scared the deer. They must have seen something big or dangerous because they bolted and went running. They couldn't possibly have seen or caught our scent among the trees. We automatically got down on our bellies and watched as the deer darted just a few yards away from us. We froze like statues, trying to camouflage into the surrounding brush and trees. Just as it appeared that the deer were going to reach us, they darted in another direction and disappeared behind a small ridge.

We were speechless, and wondered about the sudden change

"There on the walls were some ancient petrglyphs."

in the deer. We thought there must have been a hungry mountain lion or something very scary that had attempted to attack them. We rose to our feet and looked toward the area where the deer had been grazing and did not see anything unusual at all, not a mountain lion nor even a bird. Nothing. Things were now becoming too strange for us to dismiss all these experiences. Something other than coincidence was at work here. My father spoke first and said, "I think we should perhaps offer a prayer for guidance and asked for protection from whatever is tracking us in these hills." My father's two older friends agreed and in our native language we all bowed our heads and prayed.

After praying, we decided to continue tracking the deer and headed in the direction of their escape. It didn't take long before we found ourselves in another canyon walking between tall stone walls.

A small stream of water bubbled out from a large sandy area which formed a shallow pool of water. All around the outer edges of this pool were green, mossy plants and deer tracks. We knew we had found a deer water hole. The only problem was that we were a long hike away from our supplies and shelter. We knew that it would be better to head back to camp and start out earlier the next morning. We climbed up and over a large pile of boulders, then hiked along the canyon wall for a short distance, then headed up and out of the canyon. We made it over the boulders with no trouble, but when we began to hike along the canyon wall, my brother called to my father to look at something on the walls. There on the walls were some ancient petroglyphs, stone pictures which were carved on the canyon walls centuries ago by prehistoric native people. These carvings were not the usual ones which we were accustomed to seeing on other walls in other canyons. These were not pictures of sun, bird, stars and lightning symbols. These were pictures of people without heads, or with the heads and arms of animals. There were pictures of owls and figures with opened mouths. My father and his friends spoke out loud, "These pictures tell that this canyon area is full of supernatural forces. The pictures of headless people mean that bad witches and animal spirits were working together to make bad medicine here many years ago." We all agreed that to get out of this canyon as soon as possible, would be the best thing to do.

We hurried our hike and soon reached the top of the canyon. We reached our camp just after dark. We got dinner going on the fire and after eating our fill, drank a few cups of coffee. Not once did we mention the weird sounds, the deer's reaction or the petroglyphs we had experienced that day. In these times it is best to not talk about such things. To do so, we believe, would call to us the dark forces. We decided at around eight that evening to call it a day and get into our sleeping bags. After placing some more wood in the fire we all stretched out, close to the fire ring. We were very tired from all the hiking of the day, and were eager to get enough rest for the next day's activities. Very soon after zipping up into our bags, we fell into a deep sleep. I must have been the last one to nod off because I remember hearing everyone's snoring before falling asleep. The next thing I remember is being suddenly awakened by a loud snapping sound coming from one of the burning logs in the fire. I opened my eyes and stared at the black, moonless sky above. I remember thinking to myself, what a beautiful sky it was, as I viewed all the stars filling the dark spaces from one vast direction to the other. Then I turned to face some movement which caught my attention in the brush a short distance from our camp. I saw what looked like a naked person crouching down on his legs staring at me! I thought that I must be imagining this because of how tired I was. I closed my eyes and rubbed them with my cold fingers. I again turned my attention to the figure in the distance and sure enough, it was still there, just staring at me. I began to get scared, thinking it might be someone who was going to rob us. I knew that my rifle was just a few feet away from me, but I would need to react quickly in order to do any good.

As I observed this person, I realized that he was the size of a child. I watched as he made a quick motion and stood straight up. That did it for me. I threw off the sleeping bag and yelled for everyone to get up as I went for the rifle. I yelled," Hey, there's a guy over here." Everyone reacted quickly by jumping out of their sleeping bags. I told them about the person I had seen in the bushes. My father listened to me and then said,"I had been seeing that guy for some time before you woke us. There are other spirits with him as well. I've been seeing two more of them moving from juniper bush to juniper bush." This got my brother a bit scared. He spoke: "Well what are we going to do. Will they hurt us, do they want us to leave this place?" My father's friend responded: "I think we should pack up and leave this place. These are not good spirits. We saw the pictures on the rocks; those are not good pictures. Those are pictures of witches and people who work with bad spirits. I really think we should leave this place tonight." We threw more wood on the fire and we got it burning brightly. We decided to take my father's friend's advice and leave the canyon that night. As we packed up our gear, I again noticed the shadows of people, or spirits, running from bush to bush. I let the rest of the men know what I had just seen. My father decided to sing a prayer and the rest of us joined in. My father's friend then ended the prayer by announcing, in the direction of the spirits, that the creator was watching over our well-being and that they should leave us alone. Suddenly, we heard the low sound of laughter and hoofbeats leave our camp. This is when I knew our power of prayer helped us chase away what ever was watching us.

We all got in our trucks and drove home that night. We did not speak again about our experience until the next morning. During breakfast we told our mother about our experience. She said that during the day and night we were gone, an owl had been making hooting sounds in the tree in our front yard. This was very unusual and she knew that this was an omen that something bad was happening to us. She herself began to pray for us to return safely home. Aside from this experience I have had a couple more that have taken place, but I don't think I'd like to talk anymore about this.

TOHONO O'ODHAM

The Tohono O'odham, or "Papagos," as they were named prior to 1980, presently exist on a reservation which extends over a hundred miles following the Arizona and Mexican border. This reservation is also the second-largest in the U.S. It begins north in the Casa Grande area, east in the Aguirre Valley, west in the Sand Tank/Sauceda Mountains, and then ends south in Old Mexico, where a small population of Tohono O'odham presently reside in the state of Sonora. They still practice much of the traditional ceremonies and beliefs that were alive prior to contact with Spanish missionaries in the late 17th Century. The People chose to renounce the name "Papago" which means "Bean Eaters," for the more appropriate and suitable name that they have always called themselves, Tohono O'odham. The Tohono O'odham are a true desert-farming people. In years past, they used a "dry farming" technology (like the Hopi to the north) which utilized the infrequent thunderstorms and rains that flooded the washes and valleys. They planted traditional seed crops in these areas and simply waited as the earth's wet season provided the needed moisture for germination. Presently, these farming practices are no longer in use by the people and, instead, they utilize water provided by modern wells.

San Javier Del Bac Mission

An Italian Jesuit missionary named Father Eusebio Francisco Kino made contact with the the Tohono O'odham in the year 1687. This meeting changed the culture of the Tohono O'odham forever. New crops and domesticated animals were introduced, as was a new political system and religion, Catholicism. Today, church structures remain as evidence of this legacy. The Tohono O'odham provided the prime labor and artists who built all these beautiful buildings. The joint knowledge of the Tohono O'odham and Europeans regarding construction and design is admirable and will for all time be deserving of notable recognition.

David War Staff's Story

It was February in the year 1991 when I had my experience with a ghost. I was seventeen years old at the time. One saturday evening in Phoenix my high school was having a basketball game, and after the game my cousin Ralph and I left the school gymnasium at around 10 pm.

My cousin is from Tohono O'dham and I was going to spend the weekend with my aunt's family. Like myself, my aunt is Yaqui. She married a Tohono O'dham man some years ago and had two kids. One is my cousin Ralph. We got on interstate 10 and then switched on to south highway 15 for the drive to the town of Sells on the Tohono O'dham reservation. About 40 minutes into our drive we were deep in the desert. Because my car needed new tires, I had to drive just below the speed limit. The threads were just about completely worn out. I guess I had the type of car that we Indians call an "Indian Car." It was a pretty beat-up looking car, but it got me where I wanted to go. Anyway, there we were driving in the middle of the desert with the CD player going, and the darkness all around. Suddenly, a large javalina crossed the road, and I hit that wild pig with a big-old "bang!" I didn't have time think about stepping on the brakes because one second there was just the road before us, and the next there was this javalina. I knew we had some big trouble with the car because the radiator began to hiss and steam began pouring out. I immediately drove to the side of the road, and stopped the car to check on the damage. Sure enough, that animal had hit the front grill head-on, and a piece of metal had punctured my car's radiator.

Directly behind the car in the darkness we could hear the pig loudly squealing. It was a weird experience to be alone at night in the desert and to hear the dying sounds of an animal just a few yards away. It kept up the terrible squealing sound for a long, long time. I had a flashlight, but I sure wasn't going to go check on its injuries without a gun. I know that javalinas can give a nasty bite when cornered or injured. My cousin said, "You know, with a busted radiator, we're not going to be able to go any further tonight." "Yeah," I answered, "We're going to have to spend a cold night in the car, or else start walking and hope someone picks us up." We decided to stay with the car, open up the hood and hopefully, if anyone driving by saw us, they might give us a lift. After about a half hour, the javalina stopped crying. As we sat in the front seat, we waited and waited for a passing car. A few passed by, but none stopped. I looked at my watch, the time was 12:10 am. Aside from being cold, we were both sleepy. We decided to turn off the car's radio in order to conserve the battery. At that time we also decided to go outside and sit on the car's trunk, to keep from falling asleep. We kept each other up with jokes and talking about the basketball game. After a while we ran out of jokes and things to say. We each started to yawn every few minutes. I looked at my watch, the time was 1:40 am. "Damn," I thought, "When are we going to get home."

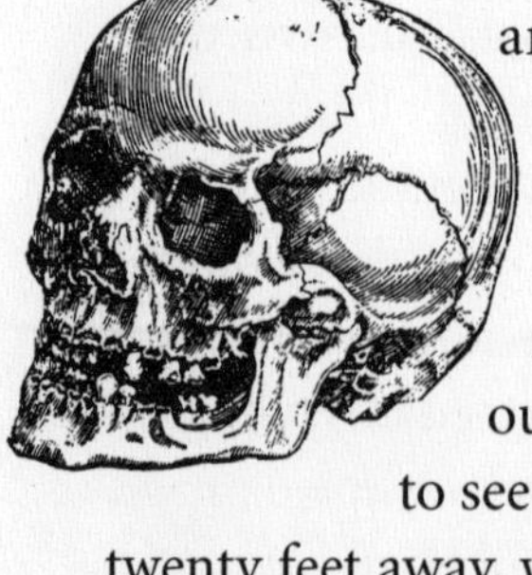

A few more minutes passed then I heard the sound of something in the bushes. I turned to looked at Ralph. I could tell by his reaction that he also heard the sound. We kept still and alert. The sound was of someone slowly walking and breaking twigs and brush with each step. The sounds were coming from the direction where the javalina was lying on the road. The moon was bright enough to make out forms in the darkness, but we were not able to see anything. Then from out of the bushes, about twenty feet away, we saw a barefoot man! I turned on my flashlight and focused the weak yellow light on him as I yelled, "Hey, what's up?" The man stopped and turned to face us. Because of the weak batteries in my flashlight and the man's distance from us, it was not easy to make out his features. I thought he was a desert tramp. There's a few of those old guys living out there. Ralph yelled out, "Watch out, we hit a javalina and its somewhere out where you're walking!" Again there was no reply from the man. Then it occurred to both of us, what's this guy doing in the desert at this hour? This was not normal. Things were becoming kind of weird. We got a little scared, then we both yelled out, "Hey, you, can't you hear us, get away from there." The man stopped, turned in our direction and looked at us. We were definitely "on the edge" at that point. I thought, if this guy has a gun, in which direction would we run? I spoke to Ralph, "This guy is some kind of weirdo, we better be careful."

Then the man took a few more steps toward the highway, and we both got a real good look at him. He was dressed in very little clothing. On his thin waist he wore a tight-fitting dark colored cloth that draped down over one knee. Around his neck were several long necklaces with large white beads or shells. He wore his hair short with bangs above his glaring eyes. One obviously strange thing was his hair. It was either greasy or wet, because when I focused the light from my flashlight on it, it shone. He was about five feet tall and very thin. He was an older man, because his face showed the signs of age. Ralph and I yelled to him, "Hey, you!" Again he did not respond. He didn't even look at us, but continued to walk across the highway and into the brush on the other side, where he disappeared. I use the word "walk," but he was floating about five inches over the asphalt! I could see his bare feet making the slow movement of walking.

As he re-entered the brush, unlike before, we didn't hear any of the twigs breaking under his footsteps. Ralph and I both looked at each other and jumped off the trunk, ran inside the car and quickly locked the doors! We knew this was no tramp. It had to be a ghost! You had to be there to feel the energy to know that this was a real ghost. What else could it have been? We spent the night, scared and hoping for a car to stop, or for the morning to quickly arrive. We were scared! We kept thinking that the ghost was going to appear to us again, only this time at the car's windows! Our imaginations kept us from sleeping. We tried to think about other things, but it was difficult not to keep focusing on the ghost. We kept the car's inside dome light on, and the radio tuned loudly to a rock station. Eventually, because were were so tired, we finally did fall asleep.

As the hours past by, sometime before dawn, we were awakened by a truck with two guys who were headed for Sells. They sure did give us a good scare when they knocked on the car's window, but soon we were introducing ourselves, and they offered to take us home. The guys told us they were artists driving from California. They were on a photography trip, taking pictures of the desert and Indians for an art project. We tied one end of a rope to the back of their truck and the other end to the front of our car, and they towed us home. We never mentioned our experience with the ghost the night before. But when we did get home that morning, we told my aunt and her family everything. Everyone agreed that what we had experienced was the ghost of an Indian from the spirit world. Since my encounter with that ghost, I've decided, if at all possible, never to drive at night through the desert again.

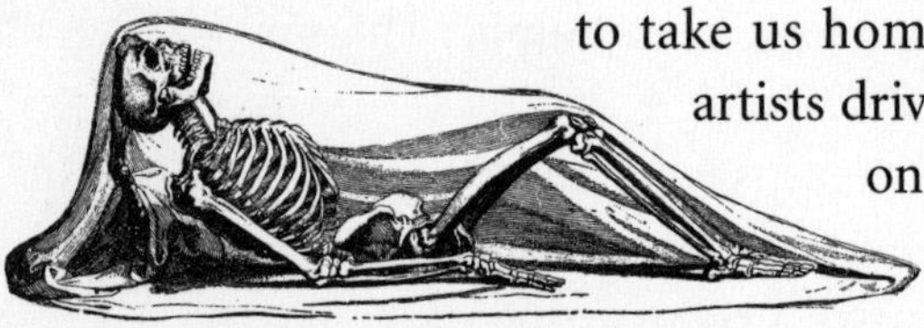

HOPI
(Hopituh)

The Hopi reservation lies within the larger Navajo reservation in the northeast quadrant of Arizona. The nearest town of Tuba City is located to the west while the largest city of Flagstaff is located to the southwest. The Hopi area itself is quite isolated by many miles of desert and canyons. Highway 264 provides the major access to and from the reservation. When mentioning the Hopi or Hopituh nation, it is difficult not to focus on such essential elements as farming and gardening. Existing and thriving in a desert environment is testament to the adaptive ability of these unique and deeply spiritual people. Hopi can trace their physical ancestral birth to their homeland as being approximately 1200 and earlier. Archaeologically, garden terraces at Third Mesa or Bacavi prove this. Farming methods used in times past are still in use to this day. Examples are the ingenious use of gardens located on mesa walls, which are irrigated terraces that are water fed by the villages located above. Another method is "dry farming." This technique involves the planting of seed within arroyos (washes) and valleys located on the lower plateaus where seasonal rain produces the moisture necessary for their germination and growth.

The Hopi cosmology is composed of four worlds, or "ways of life." At the present time, the Hopi believe that they are in the fourth way. As they moved from the third way to the forth way, they and other people were offered corn by the creator, or Ma'saw. Aside from the Hopi, all the other people eagerly and boldly took

Hopi village

the largest of the corn that was offered. The Hopi in turn were left with the shortest and smallest blue corn. The Hopi immediately knew that this was symbolic of their life to come as it too would be short and difficult. Thus, their response was to manifest the virtues of cooperation, humility and respect among themselves and others. They also knew that the earth was a wonderful and giving, living spirit and its healthiness would depend on the Hopi people as its caretakers. Today the Hopi live in four separate and autonomous mesas or villages, and within each village are sub-communities. First Mesa includes Waalpi (Walpi), Hanoki (Hano or Tewa), and Sitsomovi (Sichomovi). Second Mesa includes: Songoopavi (Shongopavi), Musungnuvi (Mishongnovi) and Supawlavi (Shipaulovi). Third Mesa includes Hoatvela (Hotevilla),Paaqavi (Bacavi), Munqapi (Moencopi), Kiqotsmovi (Kykotsmovi), and Orayvi (Oraibi).

Donald First Cry's Story

Me and my girlfriend Becky are both Hopi. I've spent most of my life on the reservation, except when I left to work for eight years in San Diego, California. My older brother and I were offered well-paying jobs as roofers in new home construction. Becky has worked at the reservation school cafeteria for just a couple of months, and we plan to get married next year. My experience with a ghost took place two years ago. Up to that time I had never had any kind of spooky stuff happen to me. I know that a lot of ghostly things do take place in the hills and mesas that surround our tribal lands, but I never really paid much attention to the stories. Anyway, two years ago Becky and I spent a summer weekend in the gambling town of Laughlin, Nevada. We never thought this short get-a-way was going to be anything but a fun time. We've driven together to Laughlin many times before without ever having encountered a ghost. So this first weird experience shook us up for a long time afterwards.

When ever we've driven to Laughlin, our normal routine is to arrive at a hotel, check into a room, then hit the "one arm bandits" downstairs. We've both done this since we were in our early twenties. Sometimes we win big, and sometimes we lose, but we have a good time nonetheless. This time, we arrived at the hotel on a Friday evening at around 7 p.m. We checked into a room on the 14th floor with a view of the Colorado River below. We emptied our suitcases of clothes, which we hung on hangers in the closet. Then we decided to watch a little television before heading to the lobby downstairs for a bite to eat. As at other times, we both knew we would spend most of the night gambling, so we were in no hurry.

As we were lying on the bed watching a comedy show, I felt an uneasy feeling come over me, a feeling of depression that I had never experienced before. I thought that maybe I was getting the flu or had gotten food poisoning from lunch. I felt a sort of a weird "thickness" come over me. I know it sounds strange, but I felt like a cold mud had covered me. I couldn't make sense of why I was suddenly feeling so bad. At one point, I looked away from the television and out the open window. Without being conscious of it, I began to think crazy thoughts of darkness covering me like a cloud. I began to shake like a leaf. My heart was throbbing and I was filled with a sense of dying. Becky must have noticed something was up, because I felt her hand touch my shoulder and say, "Donald, Donald what's the matter?" I answered, "Nothing, I'm just not feeling too good. Maybe I'm getting a cold or the flu." I told Becky that I needed to close my eyes and rest, but she looked at me funny and said, "You're drenched in perspiration, Donald, just look at you." I told her that I would be all right, but I needed to relax for a few minutes. Becky sat back on the bed, but kept an eye on me.

I turned my attention back to the television, and soon I began to feel better. Then that feeling of disaster came slowly over me once again, and I automatically began to glance out the window as before. I thought I was having an anxiety attack, because my hands began to shake and a feeling of fear began to take control of me. A friend of mine once had an anxiety attack when we were at a restaurant, so I am aware of the symptoms. I yelled to Becky, "Look at me; something is happening to me!" Becky came to my side and said, " Donald, what is it, what's going on?" After a few seconds, I decided to get up off the bed and walk to the bathroom, and splash water on my face. Becky followed, and looking at me through my reflection in the mirror, said, "Donald, should we take you to a doctor? You might be having a heart attack." I answered, "No, no let's just go get something to eat." As quickly as this thing came over me, it left. I soon regained my composure and told Becky that I was feeling much better. Whatever it was that had come over me was now gone. We decided to leave the room, go down to the lobby and get some dinner.

I began to feel much better and even got lucky when I won $800.00 playing the $1.00 slots! At about 2 a.m. we decided to call it a night, and took the elevator to our room on the 14th floor. Getting ready for bed, I brushed my teeth, then closed the drapes and got into bed. We both quickly fell asleep, but my sleep did not last for long. I was awakened a few hours later when Becky grabbed my arm and shook me hard. "Donald, Donald, wake up, wake up, there's some guy in the room!" Becky said that she had awakened with the strong feeling of someone's eyes staring at her. When she opened her own eyes she saw the figure of a young man standing next to the bathroom door. Out of fear she grabbed my arm and woke me from my sleep. I watched as Becky pointed me to look by the bathroom. At first, I didn't see anyone and then I heard a loud "thud!" It sounded like someone had fallen to the floor. I leaped out of bed and cautiously turned on the lights. As I looked around the room, I noticed there was nothing out of place. As much as I could tell, we were alone in the room. I carefully walked to the closed bathroom door, reached for the knob, and opened it. I reached inside and felt for the light switch, then turned it on. There was no trace of anyone. Although we could easily explain away the figure of the guy Becky had seen as being a bad dream, we could not explain the falling thud sound we had both heard. Throughout the night, we would hear the thud sound again and again. Being too tired to stay up any longer and discuss it further, we returned to bed and fell asleep. The next morning Becky told me she was unable to sleep and was awake most of the night.

After breakfast we walked to the parking lot, got into our car and drove to the local mall to do some shopping. We entered a dress shop where Becky began a conversation with another customer who worked in the same hotel where we were staying. She introduced herself to us and said she was a prep-cook there. The woman was a Paiute Indian from California and she and Becky hit it off right away. I excused myself, and decided to wait outside the store on a bench, while Becky had her conversation. When Becky caught up with me, she told me that the woman had given her some strange information about the hotel where we were staying. Apparently, three days before, there was a guy who had unknowingly killed himself on the 14th floor of the hotel. He was a drug addict who mixed a batch of heroin in the bathroom of his hotel room and died of an overdose. While doing her job, the maid found the body the next morning. The Paiute woman had informed Becky of this because Becky mentioned to her that we were staying on the 14th floor. Although the woman was unaware of the dead man's room number, she told Becky it was a room that had a window that faced the river below. The cook also had Becky promise that she would not tell anyone at the hotel about what she had said, for fear that she would lose her job.

Well, this new information sure did give us a new perspective. Becky became very nervous and told me she did not want to worry or scare me, but that the figure she had seen in our room the night before appeared to her once again that night. She told me that she did not get much sleep because the ghost made a sound that caused her to look in the direction of the bathroom. Once again, she spotted the ghost standing against the wall, in a leaning position. His eyes were dark black, and opened wide, and even though his mouth moved to make words, no sound came out. Then the ghost suddenly disappeared. Becky said she closed her eyes and convinced herself that what she had seen was something her imagination had made up, but she spent the night drifting in and out of sleep. With this new information, Becky and I returned to our hotel and demanded a room change. Since that weekend, we've not had another experience with the supernatural. And I have not had another anxiety attack or anything like one.

Arivaca

Arivaca, in southern Pima County about 11 miles north of Arizona's border with Mexico and mapped by Father Eusebio Kino in 1695, is in an area which contains some of the oldest mines in the United States. Arivaca, which is unincorporated, is about 56 miles southwest of Tucson. The post office was established in 1878.

The locale may have been a Tohono O'odham (Pima) Indian village before natives revolted in 1751 against the Spanish, who were attracted by precious metals and excellent grazing land. Mines developed by the Spaniards were worked by Indians under the direction of Tumacacori Mission padres. In 1833, the Mexican government approved a petition by brothers Tomas and Ignacio Ortiz to raise cattle and horses on 8,677 acres of land that formed the Arivac Ranch. (The original Indian word, "La Aribac", means small springs). Although boundaries for the ranch were never certain, its rights were bought by the Sonora Exploring and Mining Company in 1856. This company operated mines near Arivaca and Tubac. Also located on the ranch were reduction works for the Heintzelman Mine.

Charles Poston, the father of Arizona, acquired the property in 1870 and later asked the U.S. Government to confirm his right to 26,508 acres. The U.S. Surveyor general recommended confirmation of 8,680 acres, but the U.S. Congress failed to heed this recommendation. Poston's rights were obtained by the Arivaca Land and Cattle Company, which asked the U.S. Court of Private Land Claims to approve the land claim. The court refused, saying it was impossible to identify... the land which was intended to be granted. This decision was upheld by the U.S. Supreme Court on March 24, 1902, and the land became part of the public domain.

Arivaca is now primarily a retirement and residential area.

FRANCIS TORRES'S STORY

I interviewed Francis at her home. Arivaca is a small little town tucked within a quaint desert valley. Within this quiet town lies Frances's two-bedroom home. Viewing it from the street, the house would not give any indication of what had transpired just a few years ago within its walls.

Francis preferred that I not describe the outside of her house because she said that by doing so, some neighbors might identify her and start to gossip. Given her concern, I have chosen not to use her real name.

My story about El Coyote took place just a couple of years ago. I have made sure not to tell many people about what happened in the house because, being a small town, the gossip gets around really quickly. I used to rent and live in the house next to the one I now live in. I also knew the old woman who was the owner of the property. When I moved into the house next door, she and I began to talk and we became very friendly with each other. Some mornings we would have coffee in my kitchen. She sure was a talker. She told me about her son who lived in Tucson, and I got to meet him a few times before she died. I recall that the first time I visited her, she showed me around the inside of her home. I noticed that one of her bedrooms had a door with nails hammered into the door frame. Hanging on one of the nails was a small metal crucifix. I asked her about this, because it was very strange to have a door nailed shut the way it was. Her explanation was that she had nailed the door because of El Coyote. I asked her, "Who was El Coyote?" She said he was a bad spirit that needed to be kept locked up. I immediately thought that living by herself for so long made this old woman go crazy. I asked her why the spirit had the name of El Coyote. She said she had given it that name because, although she had never really seen the spirit's face, its body looked like a wild dog. I thought to myself that this poor woman needed to get out of the house more often and mingle with people.

I didn't think much more about the "friend" that she kept locked up in the bedroom. I never heard any loud noises coming from her home and, after all, she was really sweet.

One day while she was at the post office, I walked to the rear of her house and looked inside the bedroom window where she kept El Coyote. I didn't know what I would expect to see. As I looked inside, I saw a room that was without furniture. It didn't even have any rugs. Poor old woman, she must have invented this ghost as her own personal friend. I began to feel sorry for her because I myself have never married and sometimes it does get lonely. There wasn't anything unusual about the room, so I never mentioned it to her again. Well, two days later, I paid her a visit to show her a large holiday greeting card that had arrived at my house. I knocked on her front door and when she did not answer, I walked to the rear door which was left unlocked and walked inside. I immediately smelled gas. I took a few slow steps into the house and kept calling her name. There was no answer. I got concerned and quickly walked through the house. When I entered her bedroom, I found her lifeless body in bed. I called the police and they discovered the cause of her death was due to a hole in the flexible copper hose leading from the wall to her gas heater. The day before her death, she had spent the holiday in Tucson with her son and his family. I know she had died happy because, after returning home, all she did was talk to me about how nice her visit to her son's house had been.

After the funeral, her son told me that he was going to sell his mother's house. I asked him if he would sell it to me, and he agreed. I also asked him if he knew anything about the closed door that was nailed shut, and about El Coyote. He said that his mother only

mentioned El Coyote a few times, but that he thought it was an imaginary friend his mother made up. After buying the house, I had two friends who lived in the town of Nogales come to Arivaca and help me with repairs. I was overjoyed to finally own a house of my own. I began to remove old wallpaper and paint every inside wall. Of course, the first thing I did was to remove the nails on the bedroom door where "El Coyote" lived. During the repair work, I never noticed any strange noise, or saw any ghost. Except for the cold temperature that hovered in that rear bedroom, there was nothing strange at all.

Finally, after a few weeks, the house repairs were completed. After moving all my belongings into the house, I soon began to notice that the rear bedroom was strangely much colder than the rest of the house. At first, I was not much bothered by it, but it did make me wonder. At times, when I would enter the room, it was so cold that I got goose bumps on my arms. At other times, it was like stepping outside into a cool night. I thought about what the old woman had told me, but realized that perhaps my imagination was working overtime. As the weeks passed, things began to get much worse. Day and night I began to see strange shadows in the house. I don't mean shadows shaped like a person—they were more like a large blanket that covered the wall! One afternoon, I was washing dishes and I heard a strange voice. Because I was in the kitchen, I had the television volume in the living room turned up high, so that I could listen to the show. I thought that perhaps the voice was coming from the television. I stopped washing the dishes because I had a very strong feeling that someone was in the kitchen with me. I turned around to look behind me. I saw this huge black shadow—it covered the whole wall! It moved slowly, then quickly darted across the room and into the hallway. It couldn't have been the shadow of a passing car because the kitchen is located in the rear of the house.

And it couldn't have been a passing plane, because I would have heard it flying so low. No, I knew this was something that had to do with the spiritual world.

Even though I was a bit shaken, I walked into the hallway and looked in the bathroom, closets, and the bedrooms. As soon as I entered the last bedroom, a cold feeling came over me. Something told me I had to get out of there, fast! I closed the door behind me and left it closed until the following week, when a handyman paid me a visit. I had ordered a pair of new closet doors. They were delivered by a Nogales contractor who carried the new doors off his truck and into the bedroom. Everything was going fine. I was in the living room watching television as the loud noise of his electric drill started up. I remember walking to the bedroom and asking the contractor if he wanted some coffee. He said no and I left him alone to finish the job of installing the doors. Just a few minutes later I suddenly heard him yell, and as I began to get off my chair, he came flying down the hallway and out the front door! I thought he had hurt himself, so I raced out the door to meet him at his truck that was parked in the street. He was pale. He told me that "something" had taken hold of his arm. When he turned around he saw a very large man with angry eyes, grabbing hold of his upper left arm. It took all the strength he had to free himself from the ghost's strong grip. The contractor did not know anything about the bedroom, or about the woman who owned the house before I did. His experience left him shaken and I was very concerned about spending any more nights or days in the house with that "thing" walking around. I volunteered to go back into the house and return with his tools. I softly prayed to myself as I walked into the bedroom, and I guess God helped me, because I didn't see El Coyote.

After the contractor drove away, I walked back to the bedroom and placed a crucifix on the door and closed it shut, just as the woman before me had done. I decided to tell my cousin, who lives in the town just south of Arivaca, about what had happened. She asked, "If there is an angry spirit in the bedroom,

it must be protecting something. Why wouldn't it want people in the bedroom?" That weekend my cousin, her husband Pablo, and a friend came to my house to investigate. We entered the bedroom and searched the closet, and tapped on the walls. As we walked about the room, we all took turns walking over one particular spot on the floor that was colder than the rest of the room. "That's it, it's here!" my cousin said. "Whatever this ghost is protecting, it is under this area of the floor." Pablo went outside and located a small door that led to a crawl space under the house. He returned to tell us to get flashlights. The two men opened the door and they both entered the crawl space, as my cousin and I watched. Soon we heard Pablo yell to us to come outside. The men had found something. As we all gathered in the yard, they showed us a small Indian pottery bowl and some old stone beads. No money, no bones—just a bowl and beads. We placed them into a cardboard box with crumbled-up newspaper, as packing material.

I didn't want these things in my house and I decided to take them to the nearby San Javier Del Bac mission at the Pima reservation. After driving up the mission's driveway, I waited in my parked car for a moment, just to think things over. I wasn't sure if giving these Indian things to a priest would be the best thing to do. Instead, I decided to take a short drive to the reservation office and speak with someone. I met an office worker and explained to her that I needed to know if there was a person who could help me. After telling her my story, she gave me directions to the house of a woman who heals people on the reservation.

As I was parking the car on the dirt street, the woman and her son were driving up to the house. I introduced myself and quickly told her about what I had in the cardboard box. She seemed uneasy, but said she would take care of it. My meeting with her only took about 15 minutes. I know that I must have appeared very nervous, because I remember speaking to her very quickly. I opened the car's trunk, took out the cardboard box with the pot and left it on her porch.

As I drove away, I began to feel very comfortable and relaxed. Somehow I knew that I had done the right thing. A feeling of relief came over me. Since that night I have not had another experience with El Coyote in my house. Today, I use the bedroom as a workshop for ceramic figurines that I paint. I paint several different figurines of people, animals and flowers, but if you look closely you'll notice I don't have one single painted pot. I guess you can tell why I stay away from keeping pots in that bedroom!

Navajo
(Din-Neh')

The name by which the Navajo are known is not so much the name of a people as the name of a place. The neighboring Pueblo people referred to the area of the southwest that the Din-neh' occupied as Navajo. The Spanish who later arrived referred to the Din-neh' as Apaches de Navajo. This label was in time shortened to simply Navajo. Given all this excess phraseology, the Navajo have always referred to themselves as Din-neh', which means "the people," and their homeland as Dinetah'. Current usage of either two nouns is acceptable. However, it is best to use the name that the Din-neh' have chosen for centuries.

Today the Din-neh' are the largest Indian nation in the United States. Presently they account for fifteen percent of the Native American population as reported in the 1990 U.S. census. Their tribal numbers are in excess of 250,000 members. Occupying a vast area of the southwest, spreading across parts of Arizona, New Mexico, Colorado and Utah, Din-neh' land encompasses an area larger than the states of Connecticut, Rhode Island, Massachusetts, and New Jersey combined. Chinle, near the geographic center of the Navajo Indian Reservation in northeastern Arizona, is at the entrance to Canyon de Chelly National Monument. Chinle became a center for population growth and trade after 1868 when the United States signed a treaty with the Navajos. The first trading post was established in 1882, the first mission in 1904, and the first government school in 1910. Today the community, at an altitude of 5,082 feet, has been designated one of the major "growth centers" on the Navajo Reservation by the tribal government. It is an important trade, administrative, and educational center within the Chinle Chapter (a local government unit) and is headquarters for the Chinle Agency, one of five Bureau of Indian Affairs administrative jurisdictions on the reservation.

I interviewed Josie on the Navajo Reservation not far from the town of Chinle, which is located in the northeast quadrant of the state. Josie is a 41-year-old widow and mother of twin daughters aged 16. Our interview took place inside their mobile home, which is situated on deep red, rusty-colored desert land with wispy juniper trees growing in contorted shapes. Overhead is the endless vastness of turquoise blue sky.

Within such beauty, this location would be complete if not for the reality of poverty that lingered all around. As with some Native Americans, Josie daily endures such inconveniences as living without modern plumbing, electricity or heating. The interview was conducted in Josie's kitchen. On the table were various small plastic tubes and glass jars containing a rainbow of assorted tiny, brightly-colored glass beads. Josie and her daughters sew these beads onto leather and make hat bands, necklaces, earrings and bracelets. Once completed, they take these articles to local stores in town and either sell them or exchange them for personal items. Josie spoke in a calm, even tone when relating her personal experience with a witch and ghosts. Her daughters were in the adjoining living room and silently listened as their mother told me her story.

Josie Yellow Gourd's Story

My 70-year-old grandfather enjoys living in the traditional manner of us Navajos in a Navajo round house or "hogan," which is right next to our mobile home. He also prefers to speak only our native language. After my grandmother's death, he lived alone in his hogan for over twenty years. Both he and grandmother lived together in a previous hogan, but after she died, Grandfather burned their original hogan, as is our tradition to do when the owner dies. A new hogan was built for Grandfather a short time later, and this is where he now lives. About eight years ago, in the month of November, grandfather—who otherwise was in good health—began to suffer from headaches and body aches which eventually caused him to be bedridden. When grandfather's condition worsened he began to refuse food. After discussing his situation with my older brother, we both decided that it would be best to take him to a doctor in Window Rock. Grandfather was hesitant, but soon realized the logic in our decision to seek medical help. After being admitted into the clinic, he was taken through the long process of many blood tests and x-rays. My brother and I spent three days in Window Rock at a friend's house while grandfather was being cared for. When the results of the tests eventually came back from the lab, to our surprise and relief, they indicated that he only had a rise in blood sugar, which could be treated with drugs. Aside from this, his other tests were normal. Both my brother and I were still not totally convinced that all was well with him. We had seen the turn for the worse that our otherwise active and mentally alert grandfather had taken. His state of constant pain and fatigue was very unusual for him. The doctor prescribed pain medicine to help him sleep.

After filling the prescriptions we returned home. On the drive home, grandfather stated that he wanted to seek the help of a local medicine man in Chinle. Grandfather wanted to have a Sing. Among us Navajos, we have a curing ceremony which we call a Sing. The "Sing" ceremony involves the participation of an elder medicine man or woman, special songs are sung, incense is burned, and a drum and other ritual items are used. It is a lengthy ceremony and highly respected among traditional Navajos. My brother and I assured my grandfather that we would honor his wishes and contact a medicine man back home. Arrangements were made with an elderly medicine man, and a date for the Sing was set.

Four nights before the ceremony, a strange thing happened to me. It had been snowing heavily during the day, and that evening, the moon was bright and full. At around 11 p.m. I was awakened by the barking of our dog, who we keep chained to our porch. Usually she barks at skunks that live under the mobile home, or in response to the yelping of coyotes that sometimes come around our property. This time, her barking sounded different to me. It made me get out of my warm bed and walk to the window. As I parted the curtains on the front door, I saw the image of a woman I did not recognize walking about my grandfather's hogan. I reached for my jacket and boots, and walked outside. My dog was growling and barking. In the moonlit night, I spotted this strange woman as she made her way to the rear of the hogan. When I yelled at her, "What do you want?" she did not respond. I decided to confront this strange woman. With my dog still barking loudly, I quickly made my way to the hogan as my footsteps crunched noisily into the foot-deep snow. About twenty feet away from the woman, I saw that she was wrapped in a dark shawl from head to toe. Her face was hidden from my sight. Something inside me made me stop in my tracks. As soon as I stopped, the woman suddenly turned away from me. What happened next made my mouth open wide. The dark woman took off like a flash! She did not run, but seemed to float over the snow-covered ground without leaving a trace of footsteps! My dog barked and barked. I turned in the direction of the trailer and ran back. I missed a step and remember taking a hard fall. Once I reached the trailer I rushed inside and locked the door! Both my daughters told me that they had witnessed the whole affair from the safety of the mobile home window. I was out of breath and shaking. I knew that I had seen something evil outside. My girls were also shaken, and that night we all slept together.

The next day I wasted no time in telling my experience to my brother. After hearing my story, he knew that what had taken place that night had to be witchcraft. A ghost or witch had for some reason visited our home. My brother said, "Who knows how long these evil visits have been going on without us being aware of them?" We all decided that it would be best not to tell our grandfather for fear that such information would upset him, and we didn't want to risk him becoming even more ill. We also knew that this new information needed to be related to the medicine man. My brother drove me to his home, and we informed him of what I had seen. He was not surprised by my story. He said, "Oh, I know who this is." Then he explained to us that there was a Navajo medicine woman who lived not far from his house who wanted to gain a reputation in the Indian community as being a powerful spiritual person. After I heard the medicine man's description of who this woman was, I could recall her from a visit she made to my grandfather's hogan several weeks before grandfather became ill. I remember grandfather telling me that this woman had visited him because she wanted him to be her boyfriend. When grandfather refused, she got very angry at him and yelled obscenities. She left our property in a rage! The medicine man further explained, "It is difficult to gain power without earning it in the correct manner. This woman has decided to seek the help of certain animal spirits instead of asking the Creator for direction, and doing what is right." He also said, "You need to know that this woman wants to hurt your grandfather. Your grandfather refused to do what she demanded, so now she has taken revenge. She chose to make him ill, but she will not stop until he is dead." My brother and I could not understand why this medicine woman would want to be so evil as to hurt our grandfather.

Our concern now was for our grandfather to be healed. The medicine man said that he would be ready to confront this woman's witchcraft during grandfather's Sing. The night of the ceremony came and we all gathered inside my grandfather's hogan. We used kerosene lamps for light and a fire was started in the wood stove. Soon the medicine man arrived and the ceremony began. Grandfather was seated on top of a blanket which was placed on the dirt floor. In front of him the medicine man placed the items which would be used for the cleansing: a bowl of water, a leather bag of corn pollen, a basket with a beautiful eagle feather, and various other items. The medicine man began to drum and sing his songs, calling the positive forces of Mother Earth and the four directions. He sang towards the heavens and asked the Creator for vision, help, and power in defeating all evil. His singing continued for about an hour or so. He reached for the basket which held the eagle feather and grabbed hold of the feather's stem. Saying a prayer he passed the feather over grandfather's head and body. Then the medicine man returned the feather to the basket and closed his eyes. All our eyes were focused on the medicine man's face as it began to slowly change. His eyes closed tightly and his mouth began to display a severe expression of pain. His clenched teeth were very noticeable in the warm orange glow of the lanterns. I held on to my brother's arm so strongly that knew I must have left bruise marks. I was scared from watching what was taking place before us. This small elderly old man seated on the ground before us was changing into something spiritual. A force had taken over him, and what we were seeing was scaring me. Grandfather was so weak with illness that I had to brace his body with one hand so he wouldn't fall over. As grandfather closed his eyes and prayed to himself, he was unaware of the transformation which was taking place with the medicine man.

With a quick motion, the medicine man turned over on all fours, and with the gestures of a determined dog or wolf, began to crawl around, sniffing the air and pawing at the ground. Then he crawled his way to a corner of the hogan, and began to dig vigorously with his bare hands at the dirt floor. His breathing became loud and filled with energy. He dug and dug with the force of a man much younger and stronger than he. I took a quick glance at my brother. His face showed that he was also in awe at what was taking place. I returned my eyes to the medicine man who had now dug a hole about a foot deep. Then he stopped his digging and seemed to recover from his trance. In a dazed voice, the medicine man asked my brother to bring a lamp over to him, which he quickly did. Then the medicine man reached into the hole he had just dug, and to all our amazement, pulled out a soil-covered sweater which belonged to my grandfather! The medicine man said, "Here is what the witch used for her evil medicine against your grandfather, but now I will use it against her. She used this sweater as her only way to witch him. She will no longer be able to have control over him!" After saying this, he sang a song while placing the eagle feather and corn pollen over the head and shoulders of my grandfather. My grandfather took a deep breath and fell to one side. My brother was ready to catch him as he fell. Grandfather said he was tired and wanted to sleep. We left him there in his hogan covered in warm wool blankets. The ceremony was over.

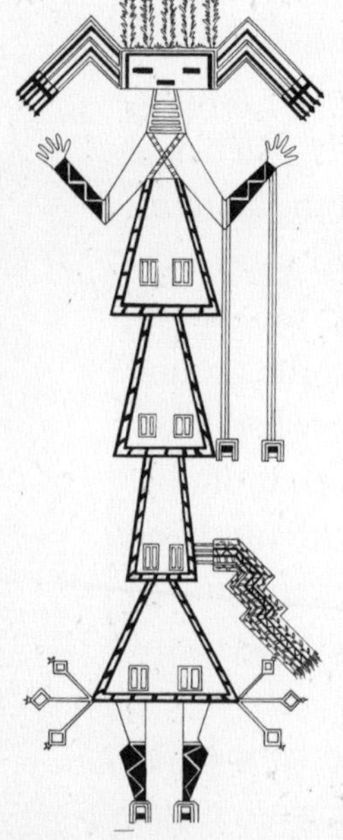

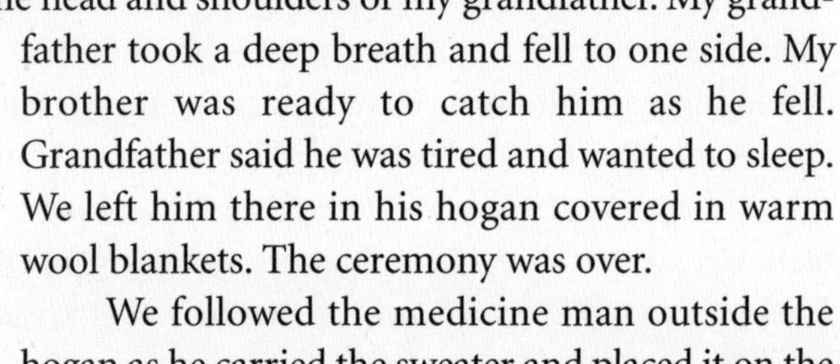

We followed the medicine man outside the hogan as he carried the sweater and placed it on the ground. He asked for a lamp, and emptied the kerosene from it over the sweater. He lit a match and tossed it on the sweater. The fire slowly began to burn and consume the sweater. Then, in the distance, we heard a piercing loud scream, a howl. We turned in the direction of the sound and spotted a ball of light which rose up high into the sky, then bounced away and disappeared into the desert! The medicine man informed us that what we had just heard and seen was the witch. "She will never be able to recover her strength, I found her power and she will be eaten up by her own evil." After that night, grandfather returned to his old self. I am convinced of the powers which some bad people can use to harm others. So much jealously and evil exits in the world. However, it is good to know that in the end, the power of the Creator always wins. I have seen it.

HOLBROOK

Holbrook is on the banks of the Little Colorado River in northeastern Arizona's Navajo County high plateau country. In 1881, railroad tracks were laid in northeastern Arizona, passing through an area known as Horsehead Crossing. The following year a railroad station was built at Horsehead Crossing and the community's name was changed to Holbrook in honor of Henry Randolph Holbrook, first chief engineer of the Atlantic and Pacific Railroad. Holbrook, at an elevation of 5,080 feet, became the county seat of Navajo County in 1895 and was incorporated in 1917. Holbrook is an important trade center for northeastern Arizona. Its location on historic Route 66 and on Interstate 40 at the junction of four major highways, between the Apache Sitgreaves National Forest to the south and the Navajo and Hopi Indian Reservations to the north, makes tourism important to the local economy.

THE NAVAJO COUNTY COURTHOUSE

This historic courthouse is located at the northeast corner of Arizona Street and Navajo Boulevard. Currently it houses the Chamber of Commerce offices and the Historical Society Museum. In 1976, a new governmental center was established south of the city. All county offices were then moved from the courthouse to this new location. In 1981 the County Board of Supervisors requested that the Navajo County Historical Society open a museum in the old building. Local residents graciously donated furniture, keepsakes and other wonderful items along with written family histories to include in the displays which are presently on view in the museum. Aside from the many notorious trials that were held in the courtroom, only one hanging took place in the courtyard on January 8, 1900, at 2 p.m.. The name of the executed was George Smiley who was hung for the murder of T. J. McSweeney.

Holbrook, Arizona, Dec 1st ~~1900~~ 1899

Mr. R. B. Berryhill

You are hereby cordially invited to attend the hanging of one

George Smiley, Murderer.

His soul will be swung into eternity on ~~*January*~~ Dec *8,* ~~*1900*~~ 1899

at 2 o'clock, p. m., sharp.

Latest improved methods in the art of scientific strangulation will be employed and everything possible will be done to make the proceedings cheerful and the execution a success.

F. J. WATTRON,
Sheriff of Navajo County.

Invitations to the hanging of George Smiley, for murder, which occurred at Holbrook on January 8, 1900. Issued by F. J. Wattron, Sheriff of Navajo County.

Revised Statutes of Arizona, Penal Code, Title X., Section 1849, Page 807, makes it obligatory on Sheriff to issue invitations to executions, form (unfortunately) not prescribed.

Holbrook, Arizona, Jan. 5th *1900.*

Mr. R. B. Berryhill

With feelings of profound sorrow and regret, I hereby invite you to attend and witness the private, decent and humane execution of a human being; name, George Smiley; crime, murder.

The said George Smiley will be executed on January 8, 1900, at 2 o'clock p. m.

You are expected to deport yourself in a respectful manner, and any "flippant" or "unseemly" language or conduct on your part will not be allowed. Conduct, on anyone's part, bordering on ribaldry and tending to mar the solemnity of the occasion will not be tolerated.

F. J. WATTRON,
Sheriff of Navajo County.

I would suggest that a committee, consisting of Governor Murphy, Editors Dunbar, Randolph and Hull, wait on our next legislature and have a form of invitation to executions embodied in our laws.

This first invitation, the news of which was sent out by the Associated Press, brought a letter of condemnation from then President William McKinley to Governor Nathan Oakes Murphy, of the Territory of Arizona. Governor Murphy severely rebuked Sheriff Wattron, and issued a stay of execution, whereupon the Sheriff sent out the second sarcastic invitation.

MARITA R. KEAMS STORY

I interviewed Marita at the courthouse, where she is currently employed as receptionist and information clerk for the Museum and Chamber of Commerce. Marita is a Navajo woman who has had numerous encounters with ghosts at the courthouse. She believes that perhaps one of the spirits that follows her around the property is the ghost of an executed man, Smiley. "I know he's around here all the time. I can feel him looking at me," she says. What follows is a detailed account of something that cannot be contained behind glass cases and roped off rooms. When the lights are turned off at the Navajo County Courthouse and all daily business has ended, another type of activity is just beginning to stir, an activity of curiously weird noises, voices, and more. Marita can tell you what she has experienced, but of course the true challenge is to experience these eerie events for yourself. The museum's hours are 8 a.m. to 5 p.m.

I've been working at the courthouse for three years, and before that I was working at the Petrified Forest National Park gift shop. I have had numerous experiences with the ghosts in the building, and I also know of others who have experienced strange things first-hand. My experiences gave me the impression that I was not welcome in the building. I guess I was being tested. Being a Navajo, we are taught that if you keep any possessions of the deceased—a shirt, furniture or whatever—the spirit of the dead person will attach itself to the item and you might have some trouble on your hands. In the museum there are lots of items of the past which are displayed in the showcases, such as old Indian grinding stones, arrows and clothing, as well as lots of non-Indian items. The museum director has informed me that some of the items that have been securely locked behind glass cases have been strangely found outside of these cases, and placed in other locations by "someone." Our museum's kitchen display seems to attract most of the activity. Utensils and other items are re-arranged to fit an unseen person's own whim for order. A museum employee named Jane refuses to open any of the display cases unless someone is with her. She keeps her own experiences to herself.

Interestingly enough, our own museum director is hesitant to be alone in the building. All our employees have experienced our names being called out from the second floor. In my case, I heard a friendly female voice, but others have heard both male and female voices calling them when they are alone in the courthouse. Another employee who was the former city tourism director had quite an experience of his own to tell. His experience happened while he and his family were driving past the courthouse one night. He noticed that the lights were left on in the second floor, when they should have been turned off. He drove his car to the rear of the building and informed his wife and teenage son that he would return after finding out who was in the courthouse at such a late hour. He opened the back door and just as he was about to enter, his wife called out to him from the car that there was a woman on the stairs on the second floor landing. This strange woman was looking out the window at them. He returned to the car and sure enough, there was a woman whom he did not recognize staring down at them. He, his wife, and son entered the building and searched for the strange woman. Although they did a thorough search, they never found her. Just a few months after I began working here, a group of kids took a Ouija board up to the third floor on a halloween night, and apparently made contact with the ghost of the building. The ghost identified himself as George. George is the name of the man who was hanged right outside the courthouse in 1900.

I was alone one evening in the courthouse when I heard a loud banging metal sound coming from the second floor. As loud as it was, I was not about to go upstairs by myself and investigate. I just

"Suddenly, I began to hear the sound of someone walking down the staircase."

remained where I was, hearing the sound. The next day, I asked a co-worker about it and he said, "Oh, the ghosts make that happen now and then." I decided not to inquirer any further. Just a few months after my first experience, I was once more in the building after locking up for the day. It was dark and I was on the second floor, standing next to a window. Suddenly, I began to hear the sound of someone walking down the staircase from the third floor approaching the second floor where I was. The doors were locked and I wasn't sure who this stranger might be. The thought crossed my mind that I could be in danger. As I kept quiet and listened for the footsteps, I noticed that they stopped.

Trying to be as quiet as possible, I listened for any sound. There was no further noise coming from the stairs. I convinced myself that perhaps my mind was playing tricks on me. After all, I had heard others speak about the courthouse being haunted. Maybe this was just my crazy imagination. Suddenly, the footsteps started up once more! I carefully made my way to the open door and peered out onto the staircase. I saw no one. I realized that I must be experiencing something ghostly. I sure didn't want to stay in the building any longer. I quickly walked down the stairs, grabbed my purse and keys and shot out the front door!

There is another event I have experienced several times during the winter: doors opening and closing on their own. Once I even witnessed the door knob of the front door of the courthouse turn, and the door open and close. We have double doors that are located directly behind the front desk, which lead out to the rear of the building. I once heard these doors swing open. I walked to the doors to investigate, and I found that the doors were locked, just as I had left them.

"This feeling is strongest in a room where an old chuck wagon is displayed."

Besides my own experiences, public visitors to the courthouse have, at numerous times, approached the front desk to tell of experiencing cold chills, or a feeling that a ghost is following them. Like these visitors, I have also experienced these same feelings. It feels like a blanket of very cold air is passing right through me. I know this sounds strange but I'm also not the only one who has experienced this. I have been told by visitors that this feeling is strongest in the room where an old chuck wagon is displayed, exactly the room where I have always felt the same thing happen to me.

Another strange unexplained thing that continues to happen in the courthouse are the faucets in the men's room that are turned on by an invisible hand. At the end of the day, I thoroughly check every corner of the courthouse, making sure that everything is as it is supposed to be. There have been several instances when I've returned after checking the men's room and found the faucets are running. I don't know who could have done this since I have been the only person in the building. I have a suspicion that it is the ghost of George. I remember another day when I was seated at the front desk and the greeting card rack began to turn on its own, then abruptly stop. I thought that there might be a small child behind it who was having fun spinning the rack. I rose from my chair and walked over to have a closer look; there was no one near it! There was also a time when, for several nights after leaving the building, I would feel the presence of someone following me to the parking lot and into my car. I felt the usual cold chills, and this presence would not leave me. I would even take frequent glances at my rear-view mirror hoping to spot something in the back seat.

At other times I'll feel the invisible hand of someone playing with my hair. I have felt my body being touched so many times that I chose not to discuss this with anyone anymore. They might even think I'm crazy. There are times when I'll be so annoyed with George's behavior that I'll yell out, "George, please stop doing this!" I won't experience any more activity for several days afterward, so I know he is paying attention to what I say. Once we had a man sent to us as a volunteer to do work at the museum. As a part of his sentence, he was ordered by the traffic court to do community work. Our employees' first impression of this volunteer was not a very positive one. This guy had heard some of the stories about our ghosts, and when he arrived for work, he began to make fun of George, and openly state that he was not afraid of ghosts. We didn't trust this worker and didn't want to leave him alone in the building unsupervised. In the museum we have a donation box and a few small, valuable things in the gift shop that would not be very difficult to steal. Well, one day I asked him to bring me some brochures from the rear of the building, where the old jail cells are located. We use these original cells as storage areas for office supplies. Just a few seconds after he left, I heard him scream. He came running to me saying that the bars and metal were making loud noises and the ghosts were trying to get him. I just smiled and giggled when he told me this. I knew that our George was keeping an eye on this guy.

The following is the deposition of T. J. McSweeney after being shot. Filed on October 4, 1899.

Question: What is your name?

Answer: T. J. McSweeney.

Question: Where do you reside?

Answer: Have been residing at Dennison.

Question: You are employed as section foreman of the Santa Fe Pacific Railroad Company at Dennison?

Answer: Yes, sir, at Dennison.

Question: What is the man's name who did the shooting?

Answer: George Smiley.

Question: What do you think caused him to commit this act? What were his reasons?

Answer: He claimed I ought to give him time check when he quit. I had to go to El Paso to have my wife's eyes treated and I asked Mr. Crowley to send man down there and this fellow worked one day for Garrity and then quit and then, of course, Garrity was the man to give him his time check. I had no more to do with it.

Question: He worked for Mr. Garrity after you had taken leave?

Answer: Yes, sir.

Question: Go ahead and tell me just what he said?

Answer: He just walked right up to me and either said, "Give me my time check" or "I want my time check," but before I had a chance to reply, came right up and struck me.

Question: What did he strike you with?

Answer: I do not know; something hard.

Question: Where did he hit you?

Answer: In the mouth and face; just one blow.

Question: What did you do then?

Answer: I started to run and he shot me in the back and I kept running.

New Mexico

Acoma Pueblo

The "People of the white rock," or Acoma, *Ah'-ku-me*, are located on a sandstone mesa 367 feet above the surrounding desert valley. Acoma is also known as Sky City, and is one the the oldest continuously-inhabited Native American villages in the United States. These pueblo people have a history of producing some of the finest examples of red-and-black-on-white pottery to be found.

The pueblo's first contact with Europeans took place in 1540. These Spaniards were initially a part of Coronado's expedition. In the year 1599 the barbarous Spanish territorial governor, Juan de Oñate, slaughtered over 800 pueblo inhabitants who were defending their homes from his forced demand of tribute and supplies. The hundreds who survived were equally brutally mistreated. Today, close to 6,000 pueblo descendants live on the reservation, and over 30 families still occupy the Sky City village year-round. Sky City Casino, owned and operated by the Pueblo of Acoma, also provides the revenue needed to develop the quality of life for these proud and historically rich people.

Roberta Whirlwind's Story

My ghost haunting happened to my mother and me on the reservation when I was nineteen years old. The last thing we ever expected to experience was a ghost. But that's exactly what took place one summer day. I remember at the time, I was in our living room watching a soap on the television. My mother was in the bedroom caring for my baby brother when our two dogs began to bark. I thought a stranger was walking up to the house. I waited for a knock on the door, but there was none. I got up to look out the window. I looked around the yard, but saw no one. Soon the dogs stopped their barking. At about an hour later, again the dogs began to bark. This time there was a knock at the front door. My mother asked, "Who's there?" and a familiar friend's voice answered, "It's me, Sonia." Sonia was a seventeen-year-old school friend of mine who lived several miles away. I got up to open the door to let her in. I asked, "Didn't you tell me you were going to Albuquerque with your father today?" Sonia answered, "Yeah, but my father's plans changed." I spotted dirt and dust on both her left leg and forearm, and her hair was also dirty. I asked her about this and she said, surprisingly, "Oh, really, I'm sorry." Sonia then turned her attention away from me and began to speak with my mother about how pretty my mother's dress was. I thought her behavior was strange because Sonia was not that much of a talker, and she never spoke to me about such things as dress patterns. I was especially suspicious of her when she began to talk to my mother about how much she missed her own mother, who had died when she was only two years old. Sonia was not the type of person who would even hint at discussing her mother's death. I know it was a emotionally painful subject for her, so I would not ever bring it up. But now here she was in my house, talking easily to my mother and me about her mother. This was too strange for me. I knew that something was not right with Sonia. I asked her if she wanted a drink of pop or water. She refused, saying, "No thanks I'm not thirsty." Again, I thought this was strange behavior because it was a hot summer day and she looked like she had been walking for a long while.

Sonia and my mother spoke for about an hour in our kitchen while I continued to watch television. I didn't feel like joining their conversation because one soap followed the next, and I didn't want to miss my stories. But soon, Sonia said that it was time for her to leave. I asked her if she wanted to wait for a ride home from a neighbor's son, who would be returning home from work in an

hour, but she refused, saying, "I need to take care of many visits before I leave to go home." I looked at my mother, who made a hidden sign to me with her head, indicating to let her go on her way. Right before Sonia left our house, she smiled, and said, "It makes me happy to see you both again. I think of you all the time." I don't remember how I answered her, but I think I said something like, "Take care of yourself, and don't fall down any more." Sonia smiled and walked out the door. My mother and I watched her as she walked down the road and disappeared in the distance. My mother spoke first, "I don't know what it is, but I got a strange feeling from Sonia. Is she doing all right? She's not on drugs, is she?" I said, "I don't think so."

I didn't hear from Sonia for two days, until I met a friend driving on the road on the way to buy some groceries. As our cars approached each other, he waved at me to stop. He told me if I had heard that Sonia and her father had been in a car accident on their way to Albuquerque, and that Sonia had died. I was shocked! I told him that she had just visited us two days before. He looked at me strangely and said, "Are you sure it was two days ago, because the accident happened at 10 a.m. two days ago." I knew that Sonia had visited my house at around 3 pm that day, several hours after the accident! I decided to keep Sonia's visit a secret, so I acted confused about the dates. I said good-bye to my friend and instead of driving on to the grocery store, I turned the car around and drove straight home. I cried all the way home. I cried so much that I had to stop the car and pull myself together. Sonia's spirit had paid me a visit and I didn't even realize it. I miss her so much. Whenever my mother and I go to church we always say a special prayer for her. It's been over seventeen years since my friend visited my house. I have not experienced any more visits or noises, or anything like a haunting. I know she is at peace, but I still miss her very much.

Santa Domingo Pueblo

The Santo Domingo Pueblo is best known because of its people's skill in jewelry-making. They produce some of the finest examples of this art to be found, and are rivaled only by their traditional art of pottery making. The native name of this pueblo is *Giuwa.* The people are friendly but generally considered the most conservative of the pueblos in terms of customs and ceremonies, which they closely guard. This cautiousness has help the pueblo maintain a high degree of religious and tribal unity.

In 1886 a disastrous flood leveled a major portion of the pueblo that included the original adobe church and homes. Four years later, the community constructed a new church, which stands today in the pueblo's central plaza. History records that Spaniards led by Oñate in 1598 and de Vargas in 1694 were intent on claiming the pueblo and its land for the Crown of Spain. Obviously, the pueblo resisted such audacity. Today, the pueblo is proud to declare its historic role against the Spaniards in the Great Pueblo Revolt of 1680. They are to be admired and appreciated.

Present day finds the inhabitants of Santo Domingo Pueblo continuing their craft work, and moving into the modern world of computers and various facets of technology.

Joseph Nightwalker's Story

My experience with a ghost took place in Santa Fe six years ago. My wife, Ruby, and I wanted to get away for a couple of days, and wanted to stay in an upscale hotel. Because of our last minute plans, we found out that all the hotels were booked up. Our second choice was to look into staying at a bed and breakfast. Santa Fe, among other things, is a city known for its excellent accommodations. An employee at The Hotel St. Francis recommended that we contact 'The Adobe Guest House' on the south of town. Ruby called, spoke to the owner, Antonio, and booked the room. The bed and breakfast was very nice. The large house had four rooms, and ours was located down a long hallway at the front of the house. During our check-in, Antonio handed us a sheet of paper that described the history of the house. Then he showed us to our room. As Ruby unpacked the suitcase, I started a fire in the corner kiva fireplace. We got comfortable and I started to read the sheet of paper that we was given to Ruby. The house was built in the early 1920s by a family named Martinez, and it was the first adobe house built in that part of Santa Fe. I read that the house was bought from the Martinez family by the first female archeologist of New Mexico, Dr. Burtha Dutton. The two men who now owned the house bought it from Dr. Dutton. I remember these details because, being an artist myself, I knew about Dr. Dutton and the stories about her association with the well-known artist, Georgia O'Keeffe. So these two names certainly are not easy for me to forget. I put the sheet of paper back on the nightstand, and my wife and I took a short nap.

About 45 minutes later, Ruby and I woke up and drove into town for our dinner reservation. After dinner it started to snow, slow at first, then harder and harder. We walked around the Santa Fe plaza, window shopping, but when we saw how heavy the snow was falling, we decided to call it a night and drive back to the B&B. When we got back to the room, I looked out the window and saw about a foot of snow covering the ground. I also noticed that there were four other cars parked in the parking spaces. There was a full house at the B&B. Ruby and I got into bed, and we quickly fell asleep at about 10 p.m.

I was awakened suddenly from my sleep when I heard the sound of breaking glass coming from down the hallway. I looked at my watch and saw that it was 3 a.m. I turned to see if the sound had also awakened Ruby. She was sound asleep. When I didn't hear any more noise, I thought that I had imagined it. I closed my eyes, and soon I heard the sound of footsteps walking down the hallway towards our room. I kept quiet. As the footsteps got closer, I heard them stop at the other side of our door. Then I heard the door knob slowly turn. By this time I was wide awake, and was fully aware of what was going on. I kept my eyes focused on the door knob, but because of the darkness, I only heard the knob turning, but couldn't see it actually turn. Then the strangest thing happened. I saw a white misty figure come right through the door! It didn't have any particular shape, it was just like drifting smoke. I decided to wake Ruby, so I hit her side with my right elbow. As she woke up, I whispered to her to look in the direction of the door. The smoke then started to change into the outline of a small woman! Ruby saw the same thing and spoke, "It's a ghost, Joseph!" Then she pulled the covers over her head. I guess I found my courage, because I yelled out to the image, "Get away, get out of here!" The ghost took two steps towards our bed. I grabbed my pillow and threw it at the ghost, then reached over and turned on the light. As soon as I turned on the light, the ghost disappeared!

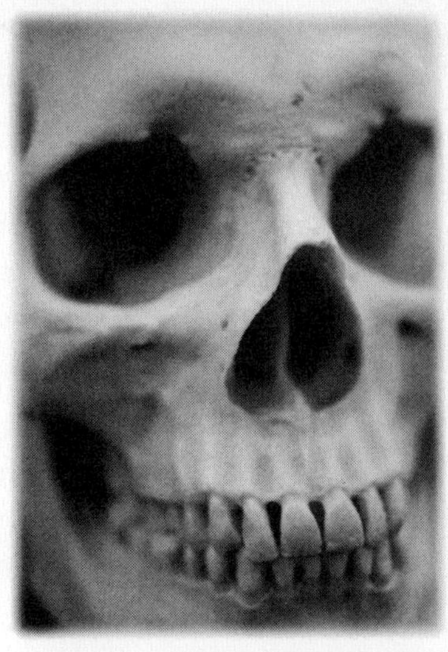

"I saw a misty white figure come right through the door!"

Both Ruby and I slept with the light on the rest of that night. In the morning at the breakfast table, I asked the owners of the B&B, Antonio and Henry, if the house was haunted. They looked at each other, then at me and answered, "Not that we're aware of. No one has ever mentioned anything about ghosts in the house. Why do you ask?" As Ruby and I told them about our experience the night before, the other guests seated at the table began to tell their own similar experiences hearing loud sounds.

Although the others didn't mention seeing any ghosts, they all said they heard the sound of breaking glass, and a few even mentioned hearing footsteps in the hallway. Ruby got nervous talking about the ghosts, and asked us to change the subject. We finished our breakfast and went back to our room. Some of the guests returned to their rooms, while others drove off to explore the sights of Santa Fe.

After a few minutes passed, there was a knock on our door. I opened it and Antonio was standing there asking if he could talk to us. I invited him in. He started to tell us a little bit more about the house. He had a nervous smile on his face, then apologized for not being totally honest with us at breakfast. As he put it, "I didn't want to upset the other guests who might be a bit sensitive about such a subject." But now he wanted to set the record straight and admit that the guesthouse was haunted, and yes, there have been several other guests who have seen ghosts in the house, including himself. He said the previous owner, archeologist Dr. Dutton, kept a collection of American Indian artifacts in one room of the house. During her many archeological digs throughout the southwest, she would return to her house in Santa Fe with stone axes, pottery, and various other samples of pueblo culture. In fact, in one room of the house she kept several medium size cardboard boxes stacked one on top of another, with actual Indian skeletons! He added that our room was not the room where the skeletons were kept, so we could feel safe about that, but that our room used to be Dr. Dutton's bedroom. He also mentioned that Dr. Dutton was still very much alive, and living in a local convalescent home. Ruby and I were shocked by this. He said that, throughout the seven years of owning the property, both he and his partner had witnessed many ghosts in the house. Antonio said there were many times when he would be in the kitchen and notice a shadow of a person walk from the hallway into the living room. He'd investigate only to discover there would be no one there. Other times he'd hear his name being called from an adjoining empty room. When he would walk to the room, he'd see the fleeing image of a shadow! Antonio's partner,

Henry, also later spoke to us about similar instances he had experienced in the house. Antonio mentioned that guests to the B&B had the common experience of hearing ghostly footsteps and the breaking sound of glass. Ruby asked, "What have you done to rid the house of these ghosts?" Antonio said that he and his 75 year old father had conducted a cleansing ritual in the entire house, and since that time, the appearances of ghosts had stopped. But now he was unsure of the reason why the ghosts had decided to return. We talked a little more about several things before he left to make the beds in the guests' rooms.

My wife and I felt a little better after having this conversation. We left to do a little shopping in town, and when we returned to the house, we noticed the faint scent of burnt sweetgrass incense. Antonio once again knocked on our door, this time to inform us that he and his father had once again blessed the whole house. That night was spent without any further visits from a ghost. The prayers and incense had chased whatever was still in the house. A few days after Ruby and I returned home to our Pueblo we got a phone call from Antonio. He mentioned that we should read the local newspaper, because on the front page was an article about the recent death of Dr. Burtha Dutton. Apparently, Dr. Dutton had died at a local convalescent home, less than a mile from her old home, now the B&B. But what we should take notice of, Antonio said, was the date of her death. She died the same night that the ghost of the white woman had visited me and my wife! Was the ghostly woman who visited us that night in Santa Fe the ghost of Dr. Burtha Dutton? I don't know how this could be proven, but we were in her bedroom, in her house, on the night that she expired. It just makes sense to us.

San Juan Pueblo

This particular pueblo has been inhabited since 1300 and is a well-known center of art. The native name is *Okeh.* The Spanish explorer Coronado first made contact with this pueblo in 1541. The ensuing years of hostility and the "harsh lash" of Spanish rule resulted in discontent and resentment. In 1680, Popay, a religious leader from San Juan, led the Great Pueblo Revolt of 1680 against the Spanish. During this revolt, approximately 400 Spanish were killed, and the survivors were driven south to El Paso. For twelve years following the revolt the pueblos lived their lives in peace. But, for several reasons, the revolt did not gain lasting unilateral support from all the pueblos. This lack of unity made a reconquest in 1692 by another Spaniard, de Vargas, possible. At San Juan, numerous ceremonies are performed throughout the year based on solar and lunar cycles. Among the more important of these dances is The Deer Dance, which assures abundance for the pueblo. This dance is performed in the month of January or February. Other important dances are the Basket, Cloud and Buffalo. Of utmost importance in these dances is the teaching of personal responsibility to the gathered onlookers.

Today, San Juan Pueblo is slowly increasing its economic base, and generating needed income with its enterprise, Okeh Casino.

Delores Thunder Cloud's Story

My experience with a ghost took place when I was only fourteen years old. My younger brother, Vincent, and I had been living in my grandparents house in San Juan. Five years before, both our parents had died when my mother lost control of their truck returning from a shopping trip to Albuquerque. They were both thrown from the truck and died at the scene. I was ten years old, and my brother was seven. We were given the choice of moving to Arizona and living with my mother's Navajo relatives, or staying in San Juan. We chose to stay in San Juan, and moved in with grandpa and grandma and their little dog, Pretzel.

Living in San Juan with my father's parents was wonderful. Grandmother had very bad arthritis that made it difficult for her to get around without help, and grandfather had a leg removed due to diabetic complications, which kept us from leaving the pueblo, but Vincent and I always looked forward to the many ceremonial celebrations that were held there year-round. We were happy and had many childhood friends. My grandparents had a two-bedroom house with a small screened porch. In the summer months, we moved grandpa's bed out to the porch, where he would spend the nights sleeping in the cool air with Pretzel lying next to him on the floor. Vincent and grandma each had their own bedrooms, and I slept in the living room on the couch.

One Sunday morning when everyone else was at church, I was taking a shower, and had left the bathroom door open. Pretzel started to bark. For some unknown reason, I felt that someone was in the house. When I looked through the hazy, glass shower door, I noticed a figure standing in the bathroom doorway. This surprised me, and I felt embarrassed. I assumed it was my grandmother and I said, "Sorry, I forgot to close the door, could you close it for me?" I saw the figure moved away, into the hallway. I said, "Grandma, is that you?" There was no response. Pretzel was barking even more. I remember feeling immediately terrified. I stood frozen and felt very helpless in the shower with the warm water falling on my body. Again I said, "Grandma, please answer me. Is that you?" When she did not answer, I decided to get out and see who was in the house. As I turned off the water and wrapped a towel around me, the thought hit me—there is a stranger in the house! I started to get scared. I thought, how was

I going to leave the bathroom and confront this person? Did he have a knife or gun? I was trembling! Somehow I got the strength to walk slowly out of the bathroom and into the living room. Pretzel came running to me with the hair on his back standing straight up, as if he were a scared cat! I looked in all the rooms, the closets and under the beds. No one was in the house, or on the porch. I returned to the bathroom and finished drying myself, then walked to the porch, sat on my grandfather's bed, and waited for everyone to return from Sunday Mass.

When they got home, I wasted no time in telling my grandparents about my experience. They listened to me, but I could tell they were thinking I must have imagined it all. Soon, I started to believe the same thing. But I never took another shower with the bathroom door open again. A few nights later, I again experienced something. This time, I knew we had a ghost in the house. I was asleep on the couch in the living room when I was suddenly awakened by the noise of someone in the kitchen. I heard the sound of dishes being moved around, then silverware being dropped on the floor. I kept still. The sounds were not very loud, they were gentle sounds, as if someone didn't want to make a lot of noise. But I could hear them very clearly. Because I was drowsy, I soon fell back asleep. Then I was awakened by footsteps coming from the kitchen to the living room. By this time I was wide awake! The footsteps were slow and they sounded as if there was dirt or sand on the floor being dragged by the shoes. The footsteps started to come over to the couch and I was scared. I closed my eyes and pretended to be asleep. The footsteps were right at the side of the couch! I could "feel" the presence of someone standing next to me. Even though I wanted to look at who was standing in the living room, because I was so afraid I kept my eyes closed tightly. Then I felt the pressure of someone sitting next to me, and one couch cushion moved as if someone had sat down. I was terrified, but still did not move a muscle. Something inside me told me that if I opened my eyes, I would be frightened to death by what I would see. In just a few seconds I felt a hand stroking my hair! I can't describe how this effected me. I was so scared that I began to softly cry. The ghostly fingers then took hold of some strands of my hair and lifted them up off the pillow. I could feel this actually happening. This scared me so much that I let out a scream and pulled the covers over my head! My grandmother yelled at me from her bedroom, "Are you alright, Delores?" In a few seconds she came into the room, and when I explained what had happened, she told me not to worry and gave me a small crucifix to hold. She also lit a candle and placed it on top of the television. The comfort of the candle's light and crucifix gave me a feeling of safety. I soon fell asleep, holding that crucifix close to me.

Well, the visit of that ghost soon became a common thing. I would experience the nightly visits at least twice a week. I knew I would be getting another visit when I would start to hear the dishes in the kitchen begin to rattle. Then the footsteps would begin, and come to where I would be sleeping. I know this might sound a little strange, but I soon got used to these visits. I never stopped being scared, but I was expecting to hear the noises. I always slept with the crucifix, and this gave me the courage to make it through another night. But one night was different. The dish sounds and footsteps started-up as usual, and as the ghost started to play with my hair, I turned over on my left side, away from the ghost, and faced the wall. Right after I did this, I felt a warm breathing on my exposed right ear. It was as if someone's lips were right next to my ear, breathing in and out, in and out! I froze. Then I heard the familiar soft words of my mother say, "I love you, Dolores." I immediately opened my eyes and turned to face whoever was in the room with me. As I did this I saw the white, shadowy image of a woman standing directly in front of the television. I knew it was my mother. Her image slowly began to fade.

I started to make out the television as it appeared behind her image. Soon she was gone. I cried and cried calling to her not to leave. But it was no use. Grandmother came into the room and I told her my story. She cried with me while she held me in her arms. Grandmother comforted me and explained the wonderful thing that had just happened to me. I never had another nightly visit from my mother again. One visit was enough to let me know she loves, and is watching over, me. Because I experienced this many years ago, I know it would be a good thing for me to now tell my personal story to others. So many people suffer the loss of a loved one. They think that they are gone for ever, but I know this is not so.

NAMBE PUEBLO

Located just north of Santa Fe, this spectacularly beautiful pueblo is known for its landscape and waterfalls. In the native language, Nambe means "Mound of Earth", or "People of the Round Earth." Although very much Hispanicized due to intermarriage with local residents, Nambe is in the process of revitalizing its cultural, traditional native life.

Spanish records note that contact with Nambe's native population took place in the early 1600s, at which time an initial church was built. That church and the following two churches were destroyed by fires, revolts or decay. Although little recorded history remains of this pueblo, the traditional Nambe arts of weaving, pottery and jewelry-making are being produced with enthusiasm and pride.

CARLOS TWO BEARS' STORY

My ghost experience took place when I was working in Albuquerque in 1992. I was working as a visiting nurse with a local hospital and had a case load of about twenty-two patients. My job was to do the usual routine of charting a patient's vitals, such as blood pressure, monitoring medications, and noting any changes related to physical and mental health. Over time, my patients grew to enjoy my visits, and I got to know them quite well. One of them was an widowed woman, Juanita, who had been living in a board-and-care facility on Albuquerque's west side. Juanita was a likable lady of eighty-two who had suffered a stroke on her left side at age seventy-seven. She had adjusted to her illness, and had made good improvements, but because she was without a family to care for her,

she had been living at the board-and-care facility for five years. The residents of this facility all had private rooms and were well cared for. The mental picture I keep in my mind of Juanita is of her wearing her favorite purple hand-knitted cap that a friend gave her on her birthday. She loved that hat, and always made sure to have it on when I'd pay my bi-weekly visits.

One day I received a sad call from my supervisor informing me that Juanita suffered a heart attract and died in her sleep. Given her age and illness, I was not surprised by the news, but nonetheless, it was difficult for me to continue my weekly visits to the board-and-care facility knowing she would not be there. The owners of the facility discovered her body in the early morning and, not wanting to alarm the other residents, kept her death a secret. The residents were told that Juanita had been taken to live with a cousin. Since the residents were for the most part incapable of much reasoning due to dementia and other chronic illnesses, none asked further questions of her whereabouts. Juanita's body was removed while all the residents were entertained in the back yard. In just two days, a new referral was made from the hospital, and a new patient, Mildred, was admitted to the facility. I, together with the facility owner, accompanied Mildred from the hospital to the board and care, and to her room. She was never told about the previous occupant, except that her name was Juanita and she had gone to live with a cousin. That was all.

The following morning when I paid the facility a follow-up visit, the administrator took me aside. She informed me that something strange had happened in the early morning to their new resident, which had shook her up quite a bit. Mildred was sitting alone in the living room watching television. I was told to encourage Mildred to talk about her "visitor." I asked her to tell me how she had spent her first night at the board-and-care. She told me a story that I will never forget. She said she was awakened in the night by someone shaking her bed. When she opened her eyes, standing next to her was a short hispanic woman. Mildred asked her what she wanted and the woman said, "You are in my bed. You need to get out of my bed and find another room." Mildred responded, "No. You're mistaken. This is my room, and this is my bed, and if you don't leave I'll call the staff!" Then Mildred said the hispanic woman waved her finger in her face and said, "This is my bed and I'm going to tell the owner how upset you've made me." After saying this, the hispanic woman disappeared! I asked Mildred, "What you're telling me is that you think you saw a ghost. Is that it?" Mildred responded, "Yes, that's what I saw. A ghost in a purple hat, and I want a room change today. I'm never going to set foot in that room again. It's haunted." I have to admit that I started to get goose-bumps. I assured Mildred that a room change would be made that day. I never disclosed any information about Juanita, or about Juanita's death, to Mildred. I definitely could see the fear in poor Mildred's eyes.

After leaving Mildred, I spoke to the administrator, and she said that she was awakened in the night by someone knocking on her bedroom door! When she got out of bed to answer the door, there was no one in the hall. Then she heard Mildred's voice yelling for help. After comforting, reassuring words from the administrator, Mildred spent the night on the living room sofa with the light on. None of the facility's residents made contact with Mildred during her admittance. There was absolutely no way she could have conjured up such a story. And what would have been her purpose? There were two other rooms available, so moving Mildred to another room would not have been a problem.

Juanita's old room was turned into an office. The staff did not want to run the risk of having another new resident complain about having an angry ghost shake their bed during the night, or being awakened by a ghost knocking on a bedroom door. All I can say is that experience in the summer of 1992 gave me a very creepy feeling that has stayed with me to this day.

History of Santuario de Chimayo

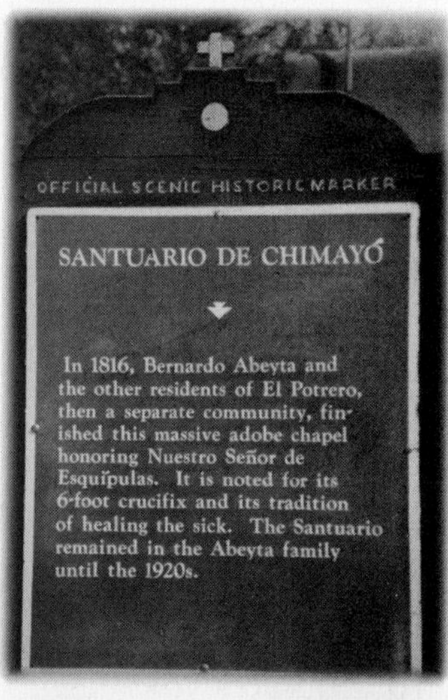

In 1816, Don Bernardo Abeyta had a miraculous vision of a light which shone from within the earth. As he brushed away the dirt, he discovered the crucifix of Nuestro Señor de Esquipulas. In time, Don Bernardo and the residents of El Potrero, then a separate community, finished the massive adobe chapel honoring the six-foot crucifix. In the rear, to the left of the main chapel is a smaller room where "El Posito" or the "little well" is located. Here, healing sand is removed by the faithful to be rubbed on the body, in hope of a cure. Adorning the walls of the Santuario are many of the cast-off crutches and personal prayers of the pilgrims who make the journey of sacrifice to the Santuario each Easter. Estimates of yearly visitors are in excess of 300,000.

Known as the Lourdes of the Southwest, the Santuario is revered by pilgrims who believe in the miraculous healing power of dirt scooped from the floor of its chapel.

Pojoaque Pueblo

In the native language, Po-suwae-geh or *Pojoaque* (using the Spanish pronunciation) translates to "drinking water place," or "gathering place." Archeological studies show the pueblo being inhabited as early as 500. In the early 1600s, San Francisco de Pojoaque, the first Spanish mission, was founded. Pojoaque was historically a major sized settlement, with a very large prehistoric population. However, following the Great Pueblo Revolt of 1680, the Spaniards, led by Don Diego De Vargas, significantly reduced its population, and it was ultimately abandoned. The pueblo was again resettled in 1706. Five families established homes and by 1712 the population increased to 79. In 1890, a smallpox epidemic combined with encroaching non-Indians once again pressured the native inhabitants to abandon the pueblo. In 1933, the pueblo was again settled by only 40 descendants of the original population. In 1936, the pueblo became a federally recognized Tribal Reservation with over 11,000 acres. Today's current Tribal enrollment exceeds over 265 members. Pojoaque is venturing its efforts into developing its economic base with several Tribally-owned businesses: Cities of Gold Casino, Poeh Cultural Center and Museum, and The Downs, a racetrack located south of Santa Fe.

Katherine Blue Water's Story

On Good Friday morning in 1987, I decided to join the group of pilgrims who make the yearly walk north to Chimayo. The night before my walk, I stayed at a friend's house in Santa Fe. I packed some snacks and two jugs of water for the walk. I figured it would

take two days of walking to get to the Chimayo Santuario by Easter Sunday. Iwoke up at 6 a.m. and walked to St. Francis Drive, which leads north to Chimayo. Groups of pilgrims were already on the road from as far south as Albuquerque. People carried home-made crosses, flowers and large pictures of loved ones. Some sang songs and some prayed the rosary. I carried my food, water, a walking stick, and a picture of my brother. I had decided to make the pilgrimage in my brother's honor. My only brother had died two days before Christmas the year before. His death was sudden and unexpected. I wanted to make this pilgrimage as my personal sacrifice to his memory.

During the first day of the walk, there were several times when I felt like giving up. It was hot and my feet were sore. But I knew I had to continue. There was just no way I could stop. I could see the determination to finish the walk on all the other pilgrims' faces as they walked past me. There were even older people on the road. I knew it must have been very difficult for them, but they were still at it. As I arrived at the area of the highway where the Tesuque Pueblo begins, I noticed that my strength was getting weaker and weaker. I walked a few more miles, and then I decided to stop at the Camel Rock rest area. I was hot, tired, hungry and thirsty. I ate and drank some of my supplies, then lay out under a shady tree and took a nap.

I had a strange dream. I dreamed that my brother was walking with me on the pilgrimage. In my dream I was unaware that he had died. We spoke to each other as if nothing unusual had happened. Another strange thing about my dream is that when I spoke to him, I was unable to recognize the sound of my own voice. It was weird. I sounded as if I were speaking in a can. My voice sounded very muffled. I also remember that, during the dream, my brother spoke to me about needing a feather for the new hat that he was wearing. I didn't recognize the hat, but he asked me to find him a nice feather. I don't know why this was so important to him, but he kept telling me to find him a feather. I attempted to respond to his words, but as I said before, my voice was confusing to me. Whenever I opened my mouth to say anything, my words came out all mixed up. When I woke up and realized that I had a dream about my brother, it made me sad, yet at the same time a feeling of happiness came over me.

Camel Rock

I got up from under the tree and continued on my walk to the santuario. This time I felt renewed, and even though I had blisters on my feet, I knew I would finish the walk. Right before nightfall, Michele, a friend of mine who was driving, located me and took me to her home where I spent the night. I told her about the dream and the strange feeling it left with me. That night I had no trouble falling asleep, and in the morning, Michele drove me back to where she had picked me up on the highway to begin the remainder of my walk. I walked for hours and hours, all the while praying to myself and thinking of my brother. It seemed to me that everyone on the pilgrimage was in a happier mood that day. Groups of people were singing religious songs and several cars were stopping, offering to give us burritos and cold drinks. Nothing unusual happened that day to me. As we had planned, my friend Michele once again located me and took me to her home for the night. I got to bed at about 9:30, but this time I had another dream of my brother. In this second dream, my brother appeared very thin and asked me to bring him water from a nearby stream. The interesting thing was that he wanted me to bring him water in his hat. He handed me his black hat and asked me to dip it in the stream, and fill it with water. I did as he asked me, but when I returned it to him filled with water, he said he could not drink the water because it was not his hat. I spoke and told him that it was his hat. He responded that his hat had a beautiful feather on the brim, and this hat did not have a feather, and therefore it was not his hat. I awoke with a dry throat. I tried to speak, but my words were very difficult to pronounce. I got out of bed, walked to the kitchen and drank two tall glasses of water. I don't know what was going on, but I knew I had to get back to sleep in order to be rested for the following day of my walk.

The next morning after breakfast, Michele again dropped me off at the spot on the road where she had picked me up. I walked and walked until I finally got to the little village of Chimayo. People were everywhere; pilgrims, tourists and locals. There must have been over a thousand people. I tried to get into the santuario, but because of all the people, I was being squeezed and pushed so much that I decided to wait for a few hours and rest under a tree, just below the hill of the santuario. It was cooler and, because I was so tired, I lay down on the grass and took a short nap. When I awoke, the crowd had thinned out and I did manage to get into the santuario, and squeezed my way into the small side room where the Chimayo dirt is kept. People bring small paper and plastic bags to fill with handfuls of dirt. I had also brought my own little bag, but I searched and searched and could not find it. I decided to use an old sandwich bag that I had in my backpack. I opened up the small bag, then reached my hand into the hole in the floor. When I dropped my fistful of dirt into the bag, I noticed something unusual. Mixed with the dirt was a feather! As I examined the feather, I knew this was a sign from my brother! I held the plastic bag up to the light and started to cry. Even though they didn't know why I was crying, people around me began to hug me. I dropped to my knees and thanked God and my brother for giving me this sign.

When I got back home to the pueblo, I told my mother about the feather and my dreams. I showed her the feather in the bag of dirt. She walked over to her bedroom closet and brought back a box. She opened the lid and pulled out a brand new, black cowboy hat. She told me that my brother had hinted to her that he wanted a hat before he died, so she and my father had bought him one, to present to him as a Christmas present. But because he suddenly died two days before Christmas, my parents decided not to tell anyone about the hat, and kept it hidden in their closet. Mother then took the bag of dirt, opened it and removed the feather. As we both started to cry, she placed the feather in the hat band and said, "Now your brother has his hat." Since then, we don't spend a Christmas without bringing out my brother's hat from the closet, and hanging it in the living room, next to the Christmas tree.

TESUQUE PUEBLO

In the Native language "Tetsugeh," means "place of the cottonwood tree." The pueblo is located just a few miles north of Santa

Fe and, despite continuous contact with European culture throughout much of its history, prides itself as being one of the most traditional of all of the pueblos. Its role in the Great Pueblo Revolt was in leading the first attack on Santa Fe. Archaeologically, the pueblo existed before 1200. Tesuque is not a large pueblo, but it more than makes up for its small size by having stubbornly resisted the Spanish and Anglo-American invaders. Traditional ceremonies continue to play an important role in the pueblo community, as does the art of pottery, which is considered very collectable. Today the enterprising Tesuque community is bolstering its economic base by focusing on tourism, gaming and farming.

DANIEL HIGH MOUNTAIN'S STORY

My experience took place in the state of California. I was visiting two old friends from high school who were living in Sacramento. Right after graduating, they moved from New Mexico to California, found work in the computer field, and got married. They always were pressuring me to follow them to California and get a job working with computers. Eventually, their phone calls and stories of making lots of money led me to drive to the west coast to see for myself. It was October, and I was planning on spending two weeks at their condo. On Halloween Eve a neighbor who was having a birthday party for a girlfriend invited the three of us over. There were about twenty or so people invited. As the evening went on, one of the dinner guests started telling ghost stories. We went around the room as each person took a turn telling a ghost story. Some of the stories were really dumb, but one guy told a couple of stories that gave us all the creeps. This guy, Randal, was involved with a group of ghost hunters. He told us about how they would go into haunted houses and graveyards looking for ghosts. The guy looked like a hippie from the 60s, long hair and beard. When he spoke he surprised me because he spoke like an educated college man. Anyway, after Randal told his stories we asked him if he had any pictures of ghosts. He said he had a three ring binder filled with pictures of ghosts in his car. We asked him if we could see them. "Sure," he said, so we waited until he returned with the photos. I didn't know what to expect. When he returned we got to see photos of fog-like images hovering over tombstones, on staircases, in homes, and in people's front yards. The pictures were taken during the day and night. Some of the photos showed the faint images of facial features, but most were just large smoky-looking forms. Randal told us that his ghost hunting group was going to be doing some research the following night, Halloween, at a local cemetery. He asked if any of us would like to come along. Most people said that they had parties to attend, but for some reason, I said that I would like to go. Normally I don't go for such things, but I told him that I would be ready for him to pick me up the next night at 9 p.m. Two others said that they would also go, so it was a date. The three of us were told to bring a tape recorder with new batteries, and a brand-new unopened cassette tape.

"I felt uneasy, but ready for whatever ghost things might take place."

The following night, we car-pooled to the Old City Cemetery on 10th and Broadway. When we walked up to the cemetery gates, I saw in the distance, among the tall stone markers, several bright lights. Randal said that his group was already preparing, and those lights were from a television crew that had also been invited. I felt a bit uneasy, but ready for whatever ghost things might take place. We were told to feel free to ask questions, and to keep an eye out for any strange movements or lights. Randal introduced us to the members of his group. Some of his friends showed us sensitive recording instruments that were supposed to measure electromagnetic fields and energy disturbances. Randal asked us to get our recorders ready. I unwrapped my tape and checked the batteries. Everything was working. Randal then asked us to walk among the graves and find a quiet spot where we "felt energy." Once at the spot, we were to turn on the tape recorder and walk away. I felt strange doing this. I located an old, fancy looking gravestone under a big pine tree, and turned on my recorder, then placed it on the grave, and walked away. I didn't feel any "energy"; it was just a grave I chose at random. I watched as the others looked at their meters and took flash pictures. I didn't see anything unusual. I was invited to have some coffee just a few yards away from the main area of activity. I kept my eyes on the tree where I had placed my recorder. I made sure that no one went by that area. At about 10:30 I decided to go and check my recorder. I saw that the tape had finished recording on side one, so I turned the cassette over, pressed the record button, and walked away. After another hour, I picked-up my recorder and brought it back to the area where we were all gathered. We each took turns playing back short ten minute portions of what we had recorded, but nothing unusual was recorded. When I played my tape, like the others, it was filled with silence.

Well, that was enough for me. I was kind of bored with this ghost hunting stuff. I told everyone that I was going to have to get back home. When I left the cemetery and got into my car, I put the recorder under the passenger seat and drove home. I kept thinking to myself what a waste the night had been. The next morning I got in my car and drove to a local cafe for breakfast. As I was having breakfast, I decided to go to my car and bring back the tape recorder. I had a pair of small headphones that I used, so the people sitting at the other tables wouldn't think I was weird. Like the night before, all I heard was the low hissing sound of the blank tape. But after about 20 to 25 minutes of listening, I started to hear something strange. I re-wound the tape and increased the volume. What I heard made my hair stand on end! At first the sounds were very low voices, then a long high-pitched whistle started up. The voices were so low, I couldn't make out what was being said. I know that no one walked-up to my tape recorder the night before, and I certainly did not hear such noises in the area. I was just a few yards away! After these sounds stopped, two very clear human voices started up. A female voice spoke, "No pictures. I said, no pictures!" Then a male voice said, "Get out, out, out, get out, get out!" Wow, I actually caught spirits talking! I took off my headphones, and turned off the tape recorder. It scared the you know what out of me! Each time I re-played the tape, I got more and more shaken up by the voices.

"I started to hear something strange."

I quickly finished my breakfast and drove around town trying to make sense of the recording. I didn't play it again until later that evening when my friends returned from work. Even they agreed that hearing the recording was scaring them. When I returned to New Mexico, I contacted a lawyer friend who worked in Albuquerque, and asked him if he could recommend a sound lab that could enhance the sounds on the tape. $150.00 later, I got my original cassette tape, and a new enhanced tape with all the sounds and voices in a much clearer form. I can only listen to this new tape for a few minutes without having to turn off the recorder and put it away. It's a scary thing to hear. I've been thinking about contacting Randal, but I don't believe that bothering the ghosts would do any more good.

Mescalero Apache

Far and wide the Apaches roamed over the region known today as the Southwest. They ranged from Texas to central Arizona, from far south in Mexico to the Peaks of Colorado. For centuries before the first Spaniards and other explorers, the Apache people knew the secrets of the mountains and the deserts as no other people have, before or since. Proud always, and fierce when need be, the Apaches bowed to no one except their Creator. They lived off the land, and cared for no possession except their land. The Mescaleros took their name from the mescal cactus. In earlier days the mescal, a desert plant, supplied the Apaches with food, beverage and fiber. Literally, it was their staff of life.

Apache Mountain Spirit Dancer by Craig Dan Goseym

A time of violence came to the Apaches in the last century. Before it ended, the Mescalero and other Apache bands had lost much of their Southwest empire. The Mescaleros were more fortunate than some other Native American groups, who were also dispossessed. They could still live in sight of their sacred mountain, White Mountain, which was, and remains, the source of their wisdom. Today, the Mescalero Apache Indian Reservation is located in the South Central part of the State of New Mexico, in Otero County. It was established by Executive Order of President Ulysses S. Grant on May 27, 1873. Subsequent Executive Orders and Acts of Congress have altered the area and defined the boundaries, fixing the gross area at 720 square miles of 460,661 acres, all of which is in Tribal Ownership status. The United States never specifically obligated itself by Treaty, or Act of Congress, to set apart a reservation for

the Mescalero Apache Indians. The Executive Orders that set aside these lands use the term "Mescalero Apache Indians, and such other Indians as the department may see fit to locate thereon."

The Lipan Apache survivors who suffered severely in many of the Texas wars were taken to Northwest Chihuahua, Mexico, in about 1930. They later were brought to the United States, and placed on the Mescalero Reservation about the beginning of 1903. In 1913, after the capture of the famous spiritual leader, Geronimo, approximately 200 members of the Chiricahua and Warm Springs bands of Apaches were being held as military prisoners. They were subsequently moved from Fort Sill, Oklahoma, to the Mescalero Reservation. The Mescaleros numbered about 400 persons when their reservation was established. Chiricahua and Lipan bands became members of the Mescalero Apache Tribe when the tribe was organized formally in 1936, under provisions of the Indian Reorganization Act.

Today the population of the reservation exceeds 4,000 enrolled members. Several families have relocated off the reservation, where they have found employment. Most of the tribal families live in or near the community of Mescalero, but there also are settlements at Three Rivers, Elk Silver, Carrizozo, Whitetail and Mudd Canyon.

The visitor who comes to the Mescalero Reservation today expecting to see braves and women in buckskins and blankets is likely to be disappointed. Changes have occurred in their ways of life over the last hundred years. In that time the Mescaleros, while striving to adjust to a dominant culture so different from their own, have survived stresses that might have destroyed people with less fortitude. Their adjustment to the complex ways of the white man's society is not yet complete. The Mescaleros have come far along the new road, however, and the trail should be smoother from now on. The tepee and the buckskin garments are gone from the reservation now, except for the four days over the Fourth of July holiday when the tribe observes the ancient "Coming of Age Ceremony" for Mescalero maidens. Gone, too, are the raids against enemy forces. Almost gone is the mescal gathering when the cactus is ripe for harvest. The deer hunt still takes place, but with rifles rather than bows. The Mescalero tribal members of today live in houses, shop for their food and other necessities in stores, drive to the stores in automobiles, and dress much as their neighbors do. The Native American language is largely spoken, although almost all of the Apaches speak the English language fluently. A few also speak Spanish. Typical Native American names have gradually vanished except for a few of the older generation. The Mescaleros are free to enter into marriage with whom they wish, thus the varied surnames now common on the reservation. Modern first names common to the general public are given. Tribal members work for their living, as do their neighbors. Contrary to belief, the Mescalero Apaches are not receiving an annuity from the U.S. Government. Not for many years have the Mescaleros, or any other Indians, received food, clothing or gratuity payments from the Federal Government. The Mescalero Apache Tribe owns Ski Apache, the largest, best-developed ski area in the Southwest. Also owned by the Tribe is The Inn of the Mountain Gods, a luxury resort complex. The Inn opened for business on July 10, 1975, and its reputation as one of the Southwest's finest facilities has grown rapidly. The Inn plays a major role in the economy of the Tribe, and indeed all of Southeastern New Mexico.

Alice Good Medicine's Story

Before I begin my story, I first have to tell you that this is going to be the last time I'll ever tell anyone about my experience. Apaches don't like to talk about these things, and I don't like to talk about ghosts either. I'm just going to tell this story because I think it's important for people to know that ghosts exist, and we should all be respectful of those who have passed on.

Eight years ago, my husband Casey and I bought a house from a man in the resort town of Cloudcroft. Casey works as a ranger for the Forest Service, and a fellow ranger told him about a very nice home that a guy was selling at a great price. At the time we were looking to buy a house and when we heard about this property, we decided to check it out. Casey phoned the owner and made an appointment the next day for the both of us to have a look. Following the directions the owner gave Casey, we entered a small canyon filled with tall pine trees. The house was located on three acres of land at the end of a dirt road. Just a few other homes were in the area. It was in a pretty isolated area. We found out that the rear of the property bordered the Mescalero reservation. We both wondered why the asking price for the property was so low. We spotted the house, and as we drove up to the front door, we kept saying to each other, "Why is the price so cheap; there must be something wrong with it." We met with the owner, who looked very thin and sickly. He told us that he had cancer and needed to sell the house as soon as possible because of the medical bills that needed to be paid. He gave us an inside tour of the house, but when he started to have difficulty walking, he asked us to walk outside on our own. As Casey and I toured the backyard and inspected the hot-tub, water pump and septic system, we knew there would be no question about buying the property. When we entered the house, we told the owner that we would talk to our bank that same day, and as far as we were concerned, it was a done deal.

A few weeks later, we moved into the house and began cleaning and removing trash left behind by the owner. Before we moved in, the owner told us that he was only going to remove what he could, and we could keep what he left at the house.

We found several boxes filled with old receipt books, and lots of photographs taken of women's hair styles. One box had scissors, combs and everything that a beauty shop would need. In the basement we found one big box filled with bottles of hair dye and blow dryers. We put most of these things in the pick-up and dropped them off at the Indian Employment Training Center on the reservation. I kept a hair dryer and some brand new hair curlers that were still in their original plastic bags. Casey found some tools in a crawl space, dusted them, and hung them in the garage. There were other smaller boxes that we could see with a flashlight, way in the back of the crawl space. Because of where these boxes were located, and all the dust, we decided to leave them where they were until we finished with the other more important chores. Everything else, we got rid of. We installed new rugs in the living room and the three bedrooms, then painted the whole inside of the house. The owner had left a washer and dryer as part of the sale of the house, and I had to move these away from the wall in order to paint. When I moved the dryer, I spotted some sheets of papers and envelopes that the owner must have misplaced. I picked them up and read them aloud to Casey. They were personal letters addressed to the previous owner of the house from another man, named Gary. The ex-owner of our house had been in love with Gary and these letters mentioned that Gary had AIDS. They were touching letters about Gary's illness and his battle with AIDS. In one letter Gary mentioned that he was looking forward to visiting for the Christmas holiday. There were birthday cards and other letters with poems and things like that. Casey told me to put the letters in a box and keep them for the owner. Casey said, "Who knows, he might call or pay us a visit one day."

About a month after my husband and I settled into the house, we began to feel some strange things. Casey and I always sensed that someone was in the house watching us. As we were alone in the house watching television, there were times when we would both hear a voice call out from another room. We would hear,

"Hey!" being called out to us. We would get out of our chairs to investigate who was in the house, but there would never be anyone in the rooms or in the yard. Other times I would hear my name being called, and when I would turn to look, I could see the shadow of a man stand in the next room, then quickly fad away! Casey also saw this same shadow walk from the bedroom to the bathroom one night. In the kitchen, our knifes would be removed from the wood knife block, and in the morning, I would find them spread out in the sink! In the bedroom a strange thing took place. One day as I went to look for a record album, I opened my closet door, and discovered that all my record albums were warped! Like an intense heat had melted them. The strangest of all these experiences took place one night. Earlier in the day, Casey called to tell me he was going to be late coming home. I decided to soak in the hot tub out back that night. While I was soaking away, I noticed something moving at our upstairs bedroom window. I looked up and saw a tall man standing at the window, staring down at me! This terrified me and I froze! I just kept staring at this figure until I heard Casey's truck come up the driveway. When I saw Casey come into the bedroom, I yelled for him to open the window, so that I could talk to him. When he opened the window I yelled, "Who's that guy standing next to you?" Casey looked to his left and said, "You see someone standing next to me, where?" I yelled back, "Right there. Don't you see him?" After I said this, the ghost walked slowly away from the window, and disappeared. Casey never saw anyone in the bedroom with him. I decided then and there to move out of the house. I told Casey, "That's it, the house is haunted and we're out of here!" He agreed with me, and we contacted a real estate company. By the end of the month, it was sold. I didn't want to haggle with the price, so when the first offer was made we took it!

A year later, I was driving through Cloudcroft when I decided to stop and pay the new owners of the house a visit. I was curious about what they might have experienced. I never told the realtor or the new owners about our ghost experiences, so when I visited the new owners, I acted as if I had nothing else on my mind. I met with the wife, and sure enough, our conversation soon turned from talking about the garden and pesky deers to ghostly shadows and voices coming from empty rooms. All along I acted as if this was all new to me. Then after a couple of minutes, I began to feel nervous, and I asked her if we could continue our conversation outside. I felt much safer talking outdoors. She told me that her husband was seeing shadows of a strange man, and feeling the touch of a hand, that would sometimes touch his face. She herself would hear voices calling her name, and one time she heard a noise which sounded like someone breaking dishes in the kitchen. Then she stopped, and said she was going back into the house, to bring back something they recently discovered in the basement. She came back with an white envelope and a ceramic jar. She gave me the envelope and told me to look inside. I noticed that on the outside of the envelope, the name "Gary" was written in pencil. When I looked inside I saw folded tissue paper. She asked me to unfold the tissue. When I did this, I saw that there was a lock of brown hair taped to the back of a small photograph of a thin man about fifty. I got the shivers and gave the envelope back to her. I asked her where she had found the envelope. She said that one day she was cleaning the closet shelves in the bedroom, and discovered it on the highest shelf. Before I got around to telling her about the love letters I had found in back of the dryer, she started to tell me about the green ceramic jar on the table before us that her husband had found in the basement. One day as he was in the basement, he spotted a group of small boxes in the crawl space. He used a long pole to pull them towards him. They were covered in thick dust, so he decided to carry them outside and open them in the fresh air. The first box contained old stuffed animals. The other smaller box contained the green jar. She told me the jar had a taped seal around the edge. Her husband used a knife to cut through the thick tape, and when he opened it, they found a small, clear plastic bag filled with what they thought was white sand. The bag was tied with a red cord, and a hand written label was attached to the cord. On the label was written: "Cremains of Gary Bullock." Right before me on the table was this jar, and the ashes of Gary Bullock! That was enough for me. I told the wife that I was getting scared. I needed to go and be on my way. I also told her that she needed to get rid of the jar and ashes. I said I would visit her again some time, but I've never gone back to that house again. And I never will!

Historic Santa Fe

Santa Fe, founded in 1610 by Spanish missionaries, translates to "Holy Faith" in Spanish, and is the oldest capital city in the U.S. Santa Fe is located on a high plateau at the foot of the Sangre de Cristos, "Blood of Christ," Mountains. Native Americans had been well established in the area, constructing notable structures and trade centers, centuries before europeans ventured into the region. Today this well-known city is regarded as one of the nations premier art centers.

Sofita Becera's Story

I conducted this interview with Sofita Becera in her living room, which also served as her bedroom. The simple items of decoration displayed about her home provided clues to Sofita's modest taste. Handcrafted crocheted doilies and other needlework rested upon Sofita's well-worn furniture. Placed at the foot of her yellow/green sofa was an oblong handwoven rug which Sofita's best friend, Belinda Ortiz, had given to her as a wedding present many years before. What remains dominant in my memory, however, was Sofita's religiosity. On a wooden table her deceased husband made over twenty years ago stood a statue of the Virgin Mary. In front of the statue was a small bouquet of plastic flowers, and a votive candle which flickered continuously throughout the interview.

Born on August 12, 1899, Sofita was nearing 93 years of age, but had the spunk and vitality of a much younger woman. She wore thick-lensed glasses because of cataract surgery performed eight years earlier. Sofita's story concerns a *molcajete*, a carved, stone tool developed by ancient Native American people several hundred years ago in the valley of Mexico. It is shaped like an average-sized melon with the center hollowed out. A smaller stone is used inside the hollowed-out portion of the molcajete to crush or grind herbs and spices. This stone mortar and pestle is so useful that it remains a popular tool with people on both sides of the border dividing the United States and Mexico.

A molcajete

Unlike a *metate*—a long, flat stone used by Native Americans throughout the Southwest to grind corn into a flour-like powder—the *molcajete* is rounded, bowl-shaped.

In 1921, I was twenty-two and had married Daniel the previous summer. We had a small house about two miles east of the Santa Fe plaza. In those days, two to five miles was not considered very far to travel, and those of us without horses would walk, carrying supplies of food or firewood. It was not an easy life, but the good times made up for the bad. My good friend since childhood, Belinda Ortiz, would join me at mid-day after I had done the cleaning and fed the chickens and goats. Belinda and I passed the time talking about what was going on in our neighborhood, things like who was romancing who. During one of these afternoon visits, Belinda and I went outside to rid my yard of a stray dog that was barking and chasing my chickens. Three young neighborhood boys came by, saw our trouble, and started throwing stones at the mongrel. Once rid of the dog, I asked the boys why they were so covered in dirt. They explained that they had been exploring in the nearby hills, and had discovered a small cave behind a grove of trees against the side of the mountain. They had gathered some sticks to enlarge the opening and peered inside. With the help of the afternoon sun, they saw several pots and a quiver of fox pelts containing arrows.

I told them they must have uncovered a burial site, and should not have touched or taken anything, because they must respect the dead. They listened with wide eyes, and then said they did not want to return, but they were afraid that others might disturb the cave. Belinda suggested they take us to the cave so we could help them cover it up. The boys agreed, and off we went.

About six miles into the Sangre de Cristo mountain range, on the eastern edge of the city, we crossed a small stream, and entered a grove of trees. There we found the cave. The opening was about four feet high and one foot wide. We peered inside and saw the small painted pots, a woven grass mat, and the quiver of arrows—just as the boys had described. In the back of the cave, I saw a large dark mass of fur and a bony foot protruding from underneath the fur and knew this was a burial cave. I realized that the corpse must have been a man and a hunter, because he was wrapped in a bear skin and had his hunt weapons with him. I kept this knowledge to myself as I made the sign of the cross. I turned to Belinda and the boys and said, "We will have to seal this up, so go down to the stream and bring mud and stones." While they were all busy at the stream, I looked inside the cave again. This time I saw a roughly carved *molcajete*. I reached in and grabbed the *molcajete* and the small grinding stone that lay beside it. I thought this would fit in my kitchen perfectly, so I carried it some distance away and covered it with grass and leaves. I felt it was worthless compared to the pots or the fox quiver. We diligently worked with our hastily gathered adobe building materials, and soon the sun had caused a dry, thin crust to develop on the surface of the moistened mud. We placed large branches with lots of leaves in front of the sealed entrance, and agreed that we had done a good job. I instructed the boys to return home on their own, but Belinda and I stayed behind.

After they had gone, I told Belinda about the *molcajete*. She was not very happy about what I had secretly done, but after she saw it, she agreed that it would do no harm to put it to use once in a while, after all those years lying unused in the cave.

A metate

I retrieved the *molcajete* and we went home. I scrubbed it clean of all mud, and placed it on the kitchen table to surprise my husband. When Daniel saw it, he admired its beauty, but asked nothing of its origins. Instead, he suggested I grind some chile for the following day's dinner. So the next day, I did as he had suggested and crushed some dried, red chile pods for dinner. The *molcajete* performed very nicely, but later that night, while I was sleeping, I was awakened by a loud banging sound. I shook my husband out of his sleep and told him to listen, but the sound had stopped. The next night, I was again awakened by the same sound, but this time I recognized it as the sound one rock makes as it is hit against another—a "click-click" sound. Immediately, I knew it was the *molcajete.* I got goose bumps on my goose bumps, but I kept still and eventually, after what seemed an eternity, the sound stopped.

The next morning I told Belinda about the sounds in the night. She said it was my own fault for taking what was not mine. I agreed and asked her to return the *molcajete* to the cave. She refused, insisting I should do it myself. But I was too frightened, so I carried the stone to the back of the house, and left it there beside the back door. From time to time, I would hear the familiar sound, but I dared not tell Daniel its history. I just endured the night poundings, and the guilt that would overcome me. Out of fear, I could not bring myself to return the *molcajete* to its rightful resting place.

One November night, as a soft snow dusted everything, I heard the *molcajete* again. It had been several months since the last time I had heard it, but as usual, the clicking sound awakened me from my sleep. I got out of bed, went to the back door and carefully peered through the window. I saw the freshly fallen snow glistening in the bright light of a full moon. Then I looked down to where the *molcajete* stood, and was surprised to see the

The ancient molcajete

materialized prints of a barefooted person press into the snow! The footprints slowly move away from the *molcajete* until they disappeared behind a large cottonwood tree. Although snow covered everything else in the yard, the exposed *molcajete*, which I was using as a doorstop, had been brushed clean, and fresh human footprints surrounded the *molcajete*. Since that night I have heard the clicking sounds of the *molcajete* only twice: on the day that my good friend Belinda died, and on the day that Daniel was laid to rest. But I was no longer afraid. I guess I've come to accept the spirit that dwells in or around the grinding stone as something that I will have to live with. I now consider the *molcajete* as if it were a chair or table, something taken for granted, but useful when needed. I believe this "stone friend" will stay with me, and provide companionship until I leave this world.

Author's Note: In September of 1991, Sofita suffered a massive heart attack and died at home, surrounded by her son and two neighbors. Later, her son contacted me and informed me that his mother had mentioned to him that she had wanted me to have the *molcajete*. I accepted the gift with nervous apprehension, and assured her son that I would take care of it and that eventually I would place it in a location that befits its history.

History of La Residencia

La Residencia is a seven-year-old nursing facility located at the corner of Paseo de Peralta and Palace Avenue. Prior to October 1983, the building housed the original St. Vincent Hospital, which provided for the health care needs of Santa Fe and Northern New Mexico. Many of the city's health care workers who served there believe it to be haunted, specifically nurses who completed residence work at this facility for their New Mexico nursing licenses. The following narrative is an interview with one employee of La Residencia—the Nurse Coordinator.

Loraine Baca's Story

All the nurses who I now work with and have worked with in the past are very much aware of the ghosts that dwell at La Residencia, but the basement holds its own special, grisly power. I personally can attest to this. You couldn't pay me a sack of gold to walk into that basement—day or night. When staff members ask me to accompany them to the basement, I tell them, "The day I go back into that hell, is the day I turn in my resignation!" The basement has many rooms and hallways, and it's very dark. The State Museum offices, which are located in the building next to La Residencia, use one large hallway as a storage area. Native American artifacts, such as stone tools, pottery and grinding stones, are kept in that space. I imagine these items, and others stored in large, sealed crates, have been excavated from burial sites. Considering how non-Native Americans treat living

Indians with disrespect, it would not surprise me if there were skeletal remains down there in cardboard boxes. I am convinced that there are a lot of upset spirits in that basement. Other employees have reported hearing loud banging noises and voices coming from the basement at odd hours of the day and night. No one—except for new employees—ever ventures to the elevator and presses the "B" button. In the past, the "seasoned" staff members used to initiate new employees by escorting them to the basement and leaving them there to find their way through the dark maze of hallways to the stairway—without the aid of a flashlight. The only available light would be the green glow from the Exit signs. Eventually, the initiates—pale as a ghost—would reach the upper floor, where we would welcome them.

One evening, I was selected to accompany a new nurse's aide to the basement for this eerie "rite of passage." We rode the elevator down and, arriving at the basement, I sent her off with the usual instructions: "Find the stairs and meet us on the third floor." She hesitated, then said, "I'll do it." As the elevator door squeezed shut, I shouted, "Good luck,"and then went upstairs to wait with the others. We waited, and waited. Nothing happened. The aide did not arrive within the expected time, and we began to worry for her safety. Imagining all sorts of disasters—a broken leg, a hit on the head—another nurse and I decided to investigate. Once in the basement, we called out the aide's name. No response. While the other nurse held the elevator door open, I shone a flashlight around—spotting dusty chairs, boxes and crates. Elongated shadows flickered and fluttered against the walls. I definitely wanted to be somewhere else. I called the aide again, and this time I heard a weak response. I followed the sound of her voice—down one hall, then to the left. Finally I located a room. I called to her again. "I'm here, down here on the floor," she said. She was in one of the storage rooms, crouched in the corner, in almost total darkness. She told me she had lost her way, then became confused and scared. I hugged her and she took my hand. Then I yelled to the other nurse, that I had found our missing aide.

As we turned to make our way out of the room, the beam of my flashlight caught something on one of the walls. I thought it was water, but as we looked closer, we saw that it was blood. It was fresh and it glistened in the light. It covered over half of the concrete wall and seemed to be oozing from the wall itself. I could even smell the unique, iron scent of hemoglobin. There was no doubt in my mind—this was blood! Well, after a scream or two—who's counting—we high-tailed it out of the room toward the elevator. "Press the button! Press the button!" we yelled to the startled nurse. When we reached the others upstairs, I told them what we had seen. Everyone got so scared that no one even considered the possibility of returning to the basement—ever. However, the following day, after much deliberation, two nurses talked me into taking them to the room where we had seen the blood. Down we went with flashlights in hand, along the dark hallway, my stomach in knots. We found the room, and I said, "Right in there, on the wall by the door." We aimed our flashlights, but the wall was dry—clean as sun-bleached bones. There was no trace of blood on the wall or on the floor. I remember saying, "Let's get the hell out of this place!" Two days later, I asked one of the maintenance men, who had worked in the facility when it was St. Vincent's, if he was aware of any strange happenings in the basement. He told me he had heard stories from other employees, but didn't pay them any mind. When I asked him about the room where I had seen the blood, he told me there used to be a small furnace in that room where the hospital surgery department cremated amputated limbs and organs. I just about died on the spot.

As you may have guessed, there have been no more initiations in the basement.

HISTORIC TAOS

There is evidence that man has lived in the Taos area as far back as 3,000 B.C. Prehistoric ruins dating from 900 A.D. can be seen throughout the Taos Valley. The Pueblo of Taos remains the link from these early inhabitants of the valley to the still-living native culture.

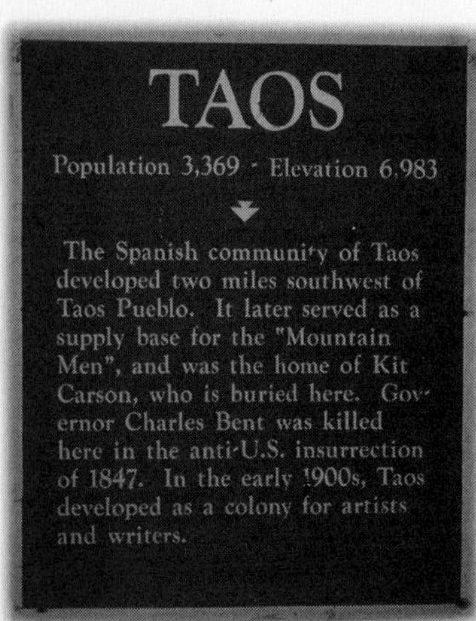

The first Europeans to appear in Taos Valley were led by Captain Alvarado, who was exploring the area for the Coronado expedition of 1540. Don Juan de Oñate, official colonizer of the province of Nuevo Mexico, came to Taos in July 1598. In September of that year he assigned Fray Francisco de Zamora to serve the Taos and Picuris Pueblos.

Long established trading networks at Taos Pueblo, plus its mission and the abundant water and timber of the valley, attracted early Spanish settlers. Life was not easy for the newcomers, and there were several conflicts with Taos Pueblo before the Pueblo revolt of 1680 in which all Spaniards and their priests were either killed or driven from the province. In 1692 Don Diego de Vargas made a successful military reconquest of New Mexico and in 1693 he returned to re-colonize the province. In 1694 he raided Taos Pueblo when it refused to provide corn for his starving settlers in Santa Fe.

Taos Pueblo revolted again in 1696, and De Vargas came for the third time to put down the rebellion. Thereafter, Taos and most of the other Rio Grande Pueblos remained allies of Spain and later of Mexico when it won its independence in 1821. During this long period the famous Taos Trade Fairs grew in importance so that even the annual caravan to Chihuahua delayed its departure until after the Taos Fair, held in July or August. The first French traders, led by the Mallette brothers, attended the Taos Fair in 1739.

By 1760, the population of Taos Valley had decreased because of the fierce attacks by plains Indians. Many times the Spanish settlers had to move into houses at Taos Pueblo for protection from these raiders. In 1779, Colonel de Anza returned through Taos from Colorado, where he had decisively defeated the Comanches led by Cuerno Verde. De Anza named the Sangre de Cristo Pass, northeast of present Fort Garland, and also named the road south from Taos to Santa Fe through Miranda Canyon as part of "El Camino Real". In 1796-97, the Don Fernando de Taos grant was given to 63 Spanish families.

By the early 1800's Taos had become the headquarters for many of the famous mountain men who trapped beaver in the neighboring mountains. Among them was Kit Carson, who made his home in Taos from 1826 to 1868. In July 1826 Padre Antonio Jose Martinez began serving the Taos parish. He opened his school in Taos in 1833 and published textbooks for it in 1834. He printed *El Crepusculo*, a weekly newspaper, in 1835 and was prominent in territorial matters during the Mexican and early United States periods in New Mexico.

After Mexico gained independence from Spain in 1821, the Santa Fe Trail became the important route for trade between the United States and Mexico. A branch of the trail came to Taos to supply its trading needs.

From 1821 to 1846, the Mexican government made numerous land grants to help settle new sections of New Mexico. During the war with Mexico in 1846, General Stephen Kearney and his U.S. troops occupied the province of New Mexico. Taos rebelled against the new wave of invaders and in 1847 killed the newly appointed Governor Charles Bent in his Taos home. In 1850 the province, which then included Arizona, officially became the territory of New Mexico of the United States.

During the Civil War, the Confederate army flew its flag for

six weeks over Santa Fe. It was just prior to this time that Kit Carson, Smith Simpson, Ceran St. Vrain and others put up the American flag over Taos Plaza and guarded it. Since then, Taos has had the honor of flying the flag day and night.

The discovery of gold in the Moreno Valley in 1866 and later in the mountains near Taos brought many new people to the area. Twinging and Red River, once mining towns, are now prominent ski resorts.

The Carson National Forest contains forested lands in the Sangre de Cristo and Jemez Mountain Ranges. It was created from the Pecos River Forest Reserve of 1892, the Taos Forest Reserve of 1906, and part of the Jemez National Forest of 1905.

A narrow gauge railroad, the Denver and Rio Grande Western, was built from Alamosa, Colorado, to twenty-five miles southwest of Taos in 1880. In later years it was nicknamed the Chili Line and eventually connected with Santa Fe. A surrey and four horses joggled passengers from the station to Taos. During World War II, the train was discontinued; Embudo Station on the Rio Grande is all that is left of it today.

The next invasion began in 1898, when two eastern artist came to Taos and depicted on canvas the dramatic mountains and unique peoples. By 1912, the Taos Society of Artist was formed by these and other artist who had been attracted to the area. New Mexico became a state in 1912 as well.

World Wars I and II came and went, and members of the three cultures of Taos—Indian, Spanish and Anglo—fought and died together for their country.

In 1965, a steel arch bridge was built west of Taos to span the gorge 650 feet above the Rio Grande, thus opening the northwestern part of New Mexico to easy access from Taos.

History of Taos Pueblo (Tua-th)

Taos Pueblo, home of the Taos-Tiwa Indians, is the site of one of the oldest continually inhabited-communities in the U.S. The name Taos is a spanish version of the native Tua-tah, which translates as "in the village." Taos Pueblo is the northernmost of New Mexico's nineteen pueblos; it is located seventy miles north of Santa Fe, the state capital, two miles north of the world-famous art colony of Taos, and some fifteen miles from the internationally renowned Taos Ski Valley. The pueblo is at an elevation of 7,000 feet.

The origin of the pueblo in its present form goes back many hundreds of years before the Spanish arrived in 1540. It goes back some 300 years before Marco Polo traveled to China in the 13th century. Had Columbus discovered the "new" world even 500 years before he did, back when Europe as we know it was young and "America" was not even a vision, and had he proceeded immediately to the great Southwest after stepping ashore on a remote island off the Atlantic Coast, he would have found in place in Taos a vibrant and established culture. The pueblo was here long before Europe emerged from the Dark Ages and made the transition from medieval to modern history. A regiment of Spanish Conquistadors from Coronado's 1540 expedition were the first Europeans to see Taos Pueblo. The Spaniards reportedly were in quest of the Seven Cities of Cibola (the fabled cities of gold) and they believed they had finally found one of the cities of gold when they saw Taos Pueblo from afar, perhaps with the sun shining upon it. What the Spaniards saw was not a city of gold but two massive, multi-storied structures made of shaped mud and straw and with soft, flowing lines which came to be the distinctive architectural style of the entire Southwest.

Taos Pueblo looked very similar to the way it does now, divided into north and south houses by the westerly flowing Rio Pueblo de Taos. In 1680 a massive revolt against the Spanish was conceived in Taos and launched successfully by the united effort of all the pueblos. The Spanish were driven back into Mexico and all of the territory of New Mexico, including the Spanish capital of Santa Fe, was again in Indian hands. This was an event truly distinctive in the annals of American Indian resistance to the opening of the "new world." It remains today the only instance where extensive territory was recovered and retained by Native Americans through force of arms. Taos, the seat of the rebellion, returned to its traditional, full independence for a period of almost two decades. The Spanish returned in 1693 with a large army, but Taos itself remained the center of open rebellion for some five years after the southern pueblos were once again subjected to foreign control. This distinctive military success is especially noteworthy in light of the fact that it was achieved by the traditionally peaceful, agrarian-based pueblos, a tranquil society that initially welcomed the foreigners with open arms.

The pueblo's native religion and culture survived not only the turmoil of the last decade of the 17th century—a hundred years before the birth of the United States of America—but also the 1847 rebellion of the pueblo against the new American government that replaced the Mexican and Spanish dominance. Taos Pueblo has retained its old ways to a remarkable degree. The rich cultural heritage of the pueblo is exemplified not only in the exquisite architecture but also in the annual seasonal dances. Visitors to the pueblo are welcomed to observe the dances, but are not allowed to take photographs of them. The current reservation economy is primarily supported through the provision of government services, tourism, arts and crafts, ranching and farming. In 1980, the Tribal Council established a Department of Economic Development to generate tribal revenue and job opportunities and to assist local Indian businesses. Many opportunities for development are available to the pueblo, some of which include increased capitalization of tourism, labor-intensive clean-industry plants, and office rentals.

Alfred J. Montoya's Story

I was born on the Taos Pueblo Reservation in 1950. The beautiful mountains which surround the pueblo are the Sangre de Cristos (Blood of Christ). They were given this name by the Spanish because, during some sunsets, the light that reflects from the sky onto these mountains colors the mountains red. These mountains are sacred to the pueblo people and are honored in a very special way. I always enjoy hiking into the mountains and being at peace with our Mother Earth. I do some hunting of deer, elk and bear, and a lot of fishing. As a member of the pueblo, I don't need a hunting license to hunt these animals; however, outside of the pueblo land it's required. I prefer to stay here in our mountains where I feel free to do as I wish without restrictions. It was in these sacred mountains where I had my first experience with spirits. In the fall of 1974, I was employed by the Forest Service. My job duty was to clean up areas where irresponsible hikers and campers had tossed paper, bottles, cans and other trash in the forest. The crew of guys I was with used horses to travel about the area. One day we were instructed by our supervisor to ride up to Blue Lake, which lay deep within the mountains, and clean up the area. I was busy with some other work at the time and was excused from heading out early. The others in my crew, including my supervisor, left in the morning, and I was to meet up with them later in the afternoon. Eventually, I reached the lake at about 3:30 p.m. that afternoon. I scouted the area and spotted horse tracks and footprints all about the ground. I knew that the crew had done their job of cleaning up the area, so I decided to head out in the direction the crew might be, in order to later meet-up with them. I had been instructed by my supervisor earlier that day to locate and follow an old crude barbed-wire fence. By following the fence, I would travel in the direction the men would be going. This was a short-cut route. I gazed above the mountain tops and noticed that the clouds were traveling fast. The cold night would soon come, so I attempted to hurry as best I could. Luckily, I had packed a few food supplies and a bed-roll on my horse before leaving for the mountains. All I knew was that the place where I would meet the others was what we called in our pueblo language, "place of the onion grass."

Ultimately, I did locate the barbed wire fence. It branched out in two directions; one went east, the other west. I sat on my horse for a few minutes, trying to decide which way to go. Trying to make sense of everything was difficult, especially since the forest was pretty thick with growth. I decided the best option was to follow my instincts and head in the direction I thought was north. I began to notice that things were not right. I knew I was getting lost because, after about five miles of riding, I began to travel down a ridge which was unfamiliar to me. To make matters worst, the sun would soon be giving way to the night, so I needed to locate my friends. Before long, I reached an area that I recognized from other previous visits to the area. Immediately I knew I had gone too far and had missed the trail. I reached a stream and followed it north. I needed to hurry because the sun was now behind a ridge and a cool breeze was settling in. Suddenly I turned to my right and I saw a beautiful big buck, about a ten pointer! The buck had his head lowered and was drinking from the stream. My horse made a noise, and the buck raised his head. He faced my direction and I could see his big, dark eyes gazing at me. I always carried a pistol with me, so when I saw this buck out in the open, I knew the opportunity for fresh deer meat was just a few feet away from me. I slowly reached for my gun, brought it into my line of sight, and had the buck in my view. Something inside me made me lower the pistol. I decided not to shoot. I put my pistol away and then looking right at those big black eyes, I held up my hand and in the Indian way said, "Good-bye my brother. We will meet again someday." As I rode my horse away, I took a short glance behind me and noticed the buck just stared at me. I soon reached the meadow area known as "the place of the onion grass." Since it was already dark, I thought it would be best to make camp for the night. I could join up with my buddies in the morning.

It didn't take long for me to make a fire and roll out my sleeping bag. I led my horse a little way to a grassy area of the meadow and left him to graze for the night. It was definitely a dark night. As I ate some of the food I had brought with me, I gazed up at the stars and felt at peace. I asked the Creator and Mother Earth to protect and watch over me. I threw more wood on the fire and listened to the cracking and snapping noises it produced as the wood was consumed. I rose from where I was seated and went to get my horse. I returned to the camp and tied my horse close to, where I could keep an eye on him. Throwing more wood onto the fire, I decided to make some coffee. There I was in the cold darkness with both hands wrapped around my coffee mug. Everything was peaceful and soon I felt sleepy enough to climb into my sleeping bag for the night. I watched the fire dance before me and very soon my eyelids became heavy. Before I closed my eyes, I heard some noise to my right. I sat up in the sleeping bag and turned my head in the direction of the noise. The flickering light of the fire illuminated the area I was looking at. There, from the forest, came into view a man dressed in old, traditional-style Indian garments. He was dancing but had his back towards me. He came closer and I kept still. He had an odd manner of dancing which I was not familiar with. Soon he was across the fire from me. Although I heard no music, no drumming sound, he danced and sang with a rhythm all his own. He danced in a backward motion. I was unable to make out his facial features because his head movements were so quick and sudden. I just saw a blur. It was very difficult to focus on his face. The song he sang was unrecognizable to me. Even the words he sang were strange. I was interested in knowing who this man was, but at the same time I was scared. It was very odd to see this man out here in the forest before me. Because of his clothes, I knew he was from another time, long ago. As he danced, he raised his arms and soon began to motion towards the darkness. He motioned as if calling someone to join him in his dance. It was strange to see this faceless man dancing and motioning as he did.

Then from the direction he was facing came another figure, a woman. She slowly entered the lit area and began to dance with the man. Unlike the man who sang throughout his dance, the woman remained silent. She danced in a forward direction, taking steps left then right, left then right. I was frozen with fear and amazement. I was as still as I could be. She was also dressed in old-style clothes. She wore traditional leggings and moccasins, and her hair was done up in the traditional pueblo woman manner. Over her back she wore a manta (a shawl worn over the shoulders and back). Although I was able to make out all the details of her outfit, her face was a blur also, and she was not someone I recognized. I kept quiet as they both danced in unison. I was mesmerized. Suddenly, they made their way away from my camp and fire and moved towards the stream. It was at this point that I heard them both laughing. They soon disappeared by the stream and into the darkness of the night. During this "spiritual performance" I was unable to move my arms, legs or other part of my body. My eyes saw the vision and my ears heard the sounds. My focus was centered in simply observing and nothing more.

After they left me, I was alone with my thoughts. I knew what I had just witnessed was a spiritual sign. I was left mentally numb. I just sat there in a void. Then again, I heard some sound coming from the north. I turned and saw what appeared to be flashlights coming my way through the forest. Great! I thought. My buddies had seen my fire and located my whereabouts! There were three lights and they moved around in the darkness, coming closer and closer towards my direction. I was so relieved and happy that they had found me. After what I had just seen, they couldn't have come at a better time. As the lights came closer, they suddenly stopped about a hundred yards away. I threw more wood into the fire and waited. Expecting to see my friends' faces any second, I sat back in my sleeping bag. Out of the forest came three male figures, three men whom I did not recognize! As they got closer I saw that they had three horses with them. When they got to about fifty yards from me, I saw that they were Indians and were dressed in white man's clothes: Levi jackets, jeans, etc. Once they were close enough for me to hear their voices, I heard them speak in mumbling tones. I was unable to make out what they were saying. As soon as they spotted me, they stood still. I don't know why or how, but immediately I knew I was being visited by more spirits once again. As soon as this thought came over me, I closed my eyes and prayed. When I opened my eyes, the men were opposite the camp fire. Then, suddenly, in an instant, they had moved to another area of my camp, horses and all! Then, in a blink of an eye, they were back where they were before, all seated and gazing in my direction.

Altogether, they extended their fingers towards me and pointed in a way that made me think I was something funny to them. They spoke, but all I could make out were mumbling sounds. At one point, one of the men bent forward to get a closer look at me. I looked at their horses and then at the fire which separated us. The man who had his eyes focused on me then let out a big laugh. I was scared.

I must have passed out because when I came to, I found myself out of my sleeping bag, on the ground, several feet away from where I had been by the fire. I was on the cold ground shivering. The last thing I remembered was being in my sleeping bag, and now here I was freezing on the open ground several feet away. I got up and walked over to where the fire was. It was out, but there were still some hot glowing coals in the pit. I threw more wood on top of the coals and soon I got a fire going again. I took my loaded pistol in one hand and a flashlight in the other and walked around the area where I had seen the three men. There was no sign that the ground or grass had been disturbed. I noticed that the sun was lighting up the sky before it made itself known above the mountains. As the light made the ground around me more visible, the only tracks I could find were the ones I had made coming into the meadow. There were no others. The grass was wet with dew and undisturbed. I soon packed up my horse, cleaned camp, and rode up the ridge away from the meadow. I couldn't erase from my memory what had happened to me just a few hours before. I was comforted by the morning sunlight that warmed my face and by the songs of the birds flying in and out of the trees.

Up in the distance I spotted my friends riding down the ridge. I heard them let out a yell and call out my name. I knew immediately these people were not spirits, but living human beings! As we met up with each other, my buddies had a shocked expression on each of their faces. "Hey Alfred, you look pretty pale," one guy said. "What happened to you?" I began to describe the night before to them. They freaked out! They were quiet throughout my story and when I was through, they began to tell me a story of their own.

They said that at about the same time that the spirits had appeared to me, they had all seen two Indian spirits! At first they heard the sound of footsteps running over the forest ground among the trees. Then a strange sense of someone watching them from the darkness overwhelmed them all. As they all sat quietly before their campfire, looking at each other, suddenly two Indian men dressed in old-style warrior outfits came out of the forest, running at full speed right by them. Of course, they all knew something unusual and spiritual was taking place. The two warriors just raced by and disappeared into the forest from where they had come. After discussing among ourselves the possible reasons for what we had all experienced, we had no answers and were perplexed. I was apparently the most puzzled of all. I guess my friends saw this and decided that I needed to have a spiritual cleansing. My friends had me face north and in the afternoon sunlight I was prayed over in the Indian way, in order to remove the bad forces I might have been exposed to. We all headed back home and did not speak about what had happened any more.

That evening, arriving at my house, I did mention my experience to my grandmother. She looked at me and listened to each word as if I was telling her something very important, something sacred. Then, after I was through, she held my hands and informed me that she had some sad news for me. I was told that my other grandmother had died the same night I had had my vision. My grandmother also told me that what I had experienced was my other grandmother's way of showing me that she was all right and was now passing into the other world, the spirit world. Grandmother further informed me that the dancing man and woman headed in a southerly direction and disappeared because, "That's the spirits' way; they travel south. Where you were is where our Sacred Blue Lake is located. It's the spirits' way." Grandmother then told me that the three men who showed themselves to me, after the two dancing spirits had left, were very different from the man and woman. "You know, those three spirits were very powerful. It was a good thing you did not speak to them. Keeping quiet was the best thing for you to do. Otherwise those spirits would have taken you away with them. You would have been left dead in the forest, your spirit would have been lifted away, and all we would have found would be your body. We would not have known what was the cause of your mysterious death. What saved you was the campfire that kept burning between where you were and where the spirits were. It was good that you asked the Creator for a blessing and for Mother Earth to protect you that night."

The story I have just told you is the truth. It is what I saw with my own eyes. There are people who do not believe in these things, but some do. I'm happy to know that my grandmother who passed away chose to let me know how she was and that she was headed to the spirit world. Because of the darkness that night, I could not recognize her. The dancing spirits were presented to me for a purpose; they were not bad or evil. But the other spirits, the three men.... Well, I knew something was not right when I saw them.

You know, there are many other stories and incidents that have taken place in and around the pueblo. I have experienced some very strange things. There are such things as witches and evil doers, but I would rather not talk about them. To talk about them would only give them more strength and increase their power for doing bad. There are areas of power up here in the mountains, areas that feel negative to the soul. Indian people whom I've spoken to have told me that, as they travel through the forest, they can sometimes feel the presence of eyes gazing at them from between the trees. Some have even told me that they feel the presence of someone following them, something that moves from behind the trees, and hides among the shadows. There are a lot of things that have happened to people around here. Most people prefer not to talk about them. Perhaps it's best not to. We'll leave it at that.

Larry C. Tibbetts' Story

The Garden Restaurant began in this building thirteen years ago. Before that it was an indoor flea market, and before that it was a grocery store. I've personally been associated with the restaurant since it began. Currently, the Garden Restaurant serves breakfast, lunch and dinner, and we have a bakery. We're located on the Taos plaza, so it's easy to locate and often a resting point while people are window-shopping or strolling through the many stores and galleries. It's also a popular gathering spot for locals and tourists alike.

It was either the first or second day after purchasing the property that I decided to take the stairs down to the basement and look around. I found the usual items that would be found in such an old building—cardboard boxes and trash. However, in one corner of the basement, there was a cardboard box which, surprisingly, contained a complete human skeleton. Pulling back the cardboard flaps, I could see the rib, hand, spine, leg and arm bones, a disorderly mass of bony framework, including the skull. The bones were surprisingly clean, although dusty. Apparently, one of the past owners of the building was into archeology. Soon afterward, when the basement was cleaned and all the trash removed, the box which contained the bones was moved to the rear of the basement and forgotten.

Two years later, the restaurant changed hands. The new owners, who were devout Catholics, took notice of the box with the skeleton and decided to have a local priest perform a blessing over the bones and bless the building. An archeologist from the local museum was also called in and revealed the origin of the bones. We were told that they were of a Native American woman. For their own reasons, the new owners named the skeleton Snowflake. After the priest was done with his blessings, the box of bones was taken somewhere in town and reburied. I've not ever had anything spiritual or unusual happen to me here in the building, but employees have. I've been told of strange noises, cold chills and other stuff happening to workers. Our two bakers, Anna and Earl, who spend most of their time in the basement where the bakery is now located, have experienced such strange things.

Anna M. Johnson's Story

I have been one of the bakers at the Garden Restaurant now for about seven months. The ghost, or Snowflake as the employees call her, has made her presence known to me in very strange ways. Although I've been scared by her, I want to think she'll never do me any harm. I hope she is a kind and friendly spirit, at least to me. I try to do nice little gestures to show her that I would like to be her friend. For instance, whenever I have any leftover dough, I will bake her her own mini loaf, and place it away from the other employees' view. I usually place it on top of a shelf and in the back away from view. Strangely, when I look for it in a few days, it will be gone. I'll then ask the others about the "missing" bread and they won't have a clue. I make these personal offerings of good will to Snowflake because I don't want her to do anything mean or evil to me. I admit that when I'm alone in the basement, the last thing I want is to have a nasty ghost watching my every move. Of course I get scared. Who wouldn't? So my little bread loaves for Snowflake are my guarantee that she will leave me alone.

I know when Snowflake is around because I'll hear strange footsteps on the ceiling above me. When I'm alone down there in the wee hours of the morning, sometimes I'll hear these footsteps. The temperature in the basement reaches between 90 to 100 degrees because of the ovens. Strangely, I'll feel the presence of someone in the basement with me. It's a freaky feeling. Then suddenly, I'll feel this bone-chilling cold wind. I'll become motionless, because I already know this is the sign that the ghost is about. Suddenly, this cold wind will pass right through me! The cold air will last about thirty seconds; then slowly it passes. I experience this about once or twice a week between the hours of 9 p.m. and 5 a.m. If someone speaks of the ghost or mentions her name, it's almost a guarantee that she will give you a dose of cold air. Because I've been talking to you about her during this interview, I know she will become excited and make her presence known to me tonight. I just know it! I'm not the only person who has experienced this. There is another baker named Earl who has heard the noises and felt the cold wind.

A couple of months ago, two other bakers and I were working in the basement when suddenly we all heard the sounds of footsteps coming from above. We stopped what we were doing, and, when the sounds continued, we looked at each other. Then, without any more notice, we heard a large metal object hit the floor above us. Boy, we were scared! The footsteps continued, only this time we heard a larger metal object being dragged as well. We all knew there was a burglar in the restaurant above us. Then we heard the footsteps become louder and louder. I grabbed a large knife that was on the table, and with the other two employees following behind, we made our way slowly but cautiously up the stairs. We turned on the lights but saw no one. We looked under every table and in each bathroom. Nothing was out of place. The doors were all locked from the inside. Immediately, we knew that the source of the noise was not due to any living person. It had to be Snowflake!

There are other times when I'll be in the basement and I'll hear the pots and pans making all sorts of noise. I'll go into the next room where they are kept on the shelves and hanging on hooks. I'll find several pots thrown over here and pans thrown over there. It's crazy. Sometimes, I'll be busy at work listening to the radio, and then I'll hear a noise, look up and see two, three, or more pans just fly off the rack onto the floor, slide across the room, and end up at the opposite wall! I know there are such things as ghosts. If I didn't know before, I sure do now. I get scared sometimes when I'm alone in the restaurant. Although Snowflake has scared me, I know she is just upset because of all the years her bones were kept unceremoniously in a cardboard box. Her spirit must be trapped within the walls of the restaurant. I just hope she finds rest and peace someday.

History of the Salinas Mission

Pueblos of the Salinas Valley

In the stones of the Salinas Valley pueblo ruins one can hear the faint echoes of the communities that lived there three centuries ago. Before they left the area in the 1670's, Pueblo Indians forged a stable agricultural society whose members lived in apartment-like complexes and participated through rule and ritual in the cycles of nature. Two ancient southwestern cultural traditions—the Anasazi and Mogollon—overlapped in the Salinas Valley to produce the later societies at Abo, Gran Quivira and Quarai. These traditions had roots as far back as 7,000 years ago and were themselves preceded by nomadic Native Americans who arrived perhaps as many as 20,000 years ago. As the southwestern cultures evolved, better agricultural techniques from Mexico and the migration of Tompiro- and Tiwa-speaking peoples from the Rio Grande spurred the growth of settlements in the Salinas Valley. By the 10th century, substantial Mogollon villages flourished here. The dwellers practiced minimal agriculture supplemented by hunting and gathering, made a simple red or brown pottery, and lived in pit houses and, later, above ground *jacales* of adobe-plastered poles.

By the late 1100's the Anasazi tradition from the Colorado Plateau, introduced through the Cibola (Zuni) district and Rio

Grande pueblos, began to assimilate the Mogollon. The contiguous stone-and-adobe homes of the Anasazis represented the earliest stage of the pueblo society later encountered by the Spanish. Over the next few hundred years the Salinas Valley became a major trade center and one of the most populous parts of the pueblo world, with perhaps 10,000 or more inhabitants in the 17th century. Located astride major trade routes, the villagers were both producers and middlemen between the Rio Grande villages and the plains nations to the east. They traded maize, pinon nuts, beans, squash, salt and cotton goods for dried buffalo meat, hides, flints and shells.

By 1300 the Anasazi culture was dominant, although the Salinas area always lagged behind the Anasazi heartland to the north in cultural developments. Brush-and-mud *jacales* had evolved into large stone complexes, some with hundreds of rooms, surrounding kiva-studded plazas.

Besides the domestic plants already mentioned, the inhabitants ate wild plants, raised turkeys, and hunted rabbits, deer, antelope and bison. They wore breech cloths, bison robes, antelope and deer hides, and decorative blankets of cotton and yucca fiber. Turquoise and shell jewelry obtained in trading were used in rituals. The Spaniards were impressed by the Pueblos' weaving, basket making and fine black-on-white pottery, a technique the Salinas people borrowed from the Rio Grande pueblos.

The Salinas pueblo dwellers were an adaptable people who drew what was useful from more advanced groups. But strong influences from the Zuni district, the Spanish explorers, and deteriorating relations with the Apaches to the east radically altered pueblo life. In the end, cultural conflict and natural disaster devastated the Salinas pueblos. The Apaches, formerly trading partners, began raiding the pueblos both for food and for revenge for Spanish slave raids in which Pueblo Indians had participated. The pueblos might have survived the raids, but along with the Apaches and Spaniards they were hit during the 1660s and 1670s with drought and widespread famine that killed 450 people at Gran

Quivira alone. Recurring epidemics further decimated the population, which had little resistance to introduced diseases. The ability of the pueblos to withstand these disasters may have been weakened by the direct disruption of their culture under harsh Spanish rule. In any event, the Salinas pueblos and missions were abandoned during the 1670s, and the surviving Indians went to live with cultural relatives in other pueblos. In 1680 the Pueblos north of Salinas, in an uncharacteristic show of unity, revolted and expelled the Spaniards from their lands in New Mexico. In the general exodus of Native Americans and Spaniards, the Piro and Tompiro survivors of the Salinas pueblos moved south with the Spaniards to the El Paso area. They were absorbed by Indian communities there, making them the only linguistic group among the Pueblo Indians during the historic period to lose their language and their homeland.

Maria de la Cruz's Story (Hispanic)

I interviewed Maria in the home where she and her husband live, now located in the city of Albuquerque. From time to time during the interview, she asked me to stop the tape recorder in order to gather her emotional strength. I could clearly see that the interview was not going to be easy for her. Maria still felt the fear of what she experienced over ten years before. The interview proceeded slowly but cautiously.

My first experience at the Salinas Mission ruins took place about ten years ago, when I was seventeen years old. My mother was going to spend the weekend with her sister and brother-in-law, who lived in the town of Mountainair. She asked me to accompany her on the trip. She knew I would enjoy the visit because I would also have the opportunity to visit with their children, my cousins.

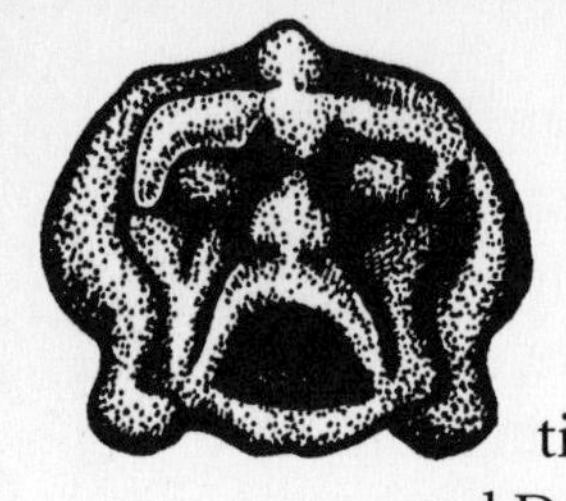

At the time, we lived just about twenty miles north of Mountainair, in the very small town of Estancia. We arrived at my cousins' house at 11a.m. My mother spent the time in conversation with her sister, and I with my cousin Delfina, and Delfina's boyfriend.

After dinner, Delfina decided that we should go for a ride in her boyfriend's car. I told my mother about the plan, and she said, "Just be back before it gets real dark." Off we went. We drove west following the setting sun, listening to music from our cassette tapes. We were having fun just cruising along. Eventually, we came to a gate and a sign that read, "Salinas Pueblo Mission National Monument." Neither of us had ever visited the monument, but we knew a little about it from our parents. We decided to stop and look around. There was a small sign that hung on a chain across the dirt road leading to the entrance that read, Closed. We decided to take a chance and left the car parked by the side of the road. We then walked over into the site. I asked Delfina and her boyfriend to take the lead. As she held on to her boyfriend's hand, I carefully followed behind. It was a warm August night and I knew from experience that on such nights rattlesnakes liked to come out of their burrows and feed. I didn't want to take any chances on getting bitten. We kept our ears open for a rattling noise. The moon was out and shining brightly, so this gave us confidence as we walked along the road. As we got within sight of the tall ruins of the church, we noticed a soft, yellow glow coming from within the structure. We thought there must be a private party for the park rangers or a celebration of some kind going on. As we got closer, we heard the low singing or chanting of church music. It wasn't very loud, but we could clearly hear it as we approached. Not wanting to be noticed, we carefully approached the front entrance of the church and looked inside.

We could not believe our eyes! There was a misty, yellow cloud that looked like fog. This fog floated about a foot or two above the ground. Above this cloud were several twinkling lights, similar to the flames of flickering candles. It was such a beautiful thing to witness that it didn't frighten us at all. We were amazed as we gazed at the wonderful sight. The chanting music slowly intensified; however, we were unable to make out the words. Then, from within the fog, we saw the ghostly images of people slowly emerge! Their complete forms were difficult to make out, but I could see their shoulders and small heads. I said, "Look, you guys! People are appearing in the cloud!" Delfina's boyfriend reached down and picked up a small stone. He took a swing and threw it. It landed within the middle of the cloud and immediately the ghostly images along with the cloud and bright light, disappeared! That was all it took to send us running back to the car. Rattlesnakes or not, I didn't care where I stepped. I was determined to be the first one to reach the car and get inside! Once we were in the car, we drove without stopping until we reached my cousins' house.

We told our parents what we had seen, and they reprimanded us for being so foolish. "You should never have done what you did. Don't you know those places are sacred? There are lots of spirits that hang around the mission, and you should give thanks to God that they did not take you with them!" Delfina's father told us about the time that he and his friend saw some ghosts at the mission when they were children. "I remember the time that my friend Luis and I were playing in an area of the mission that had some small hills. We didn't know it at the time, but those small mounds were what was left of the original pueblo houses. We heard a noise in the trees, and then a large flock of birds flew away. Suddenly, everything seemed still; even the wind stopped. Then we saw three small shadows of people running in and out of the trees. They would look at us from behind the trees, and then they would run and hide behind other nearby trees. I got the feeling that they were playing a game with us. We never got close to them because we were somewhat afraid. I was nine and Luis was ten years old at the time, and as far as I'm able to remember, the ghostly shadows weren't any taller than us."

Today, as an adult, I'll make sure that my baby is aware of ghosts, and that they should be respected. I never make fun of spirits. I know from experience that there are things we can't explain, so we should just leave them alone.

APPENDIX

Native American Graves Protection and Repatriation Act of 1990 (NAGPRA)

(PL 101-601; 25 USC 3001-13; 104 Stat. 3042)

This act was approved November 16, 1990 and in summary states:

This act assigns ownership and control of Native American cultural items, human remains, and associated funerary objects to Native Americans. It also establishes requirements for the treatment of Native American human remains and sacred or cultural objects found on Federal land. This act further provides for the protection, inventory, and repatriation of Native American cultural items, human remains, and associated funerary objects. When these items are inadvertently discovered, cease activity, make a reasonable effort to protect the items, and notify the appropriate Indian tribe(s) and/or Native Hawaiian organization(s).

As of November 16, 1995, Federal agencies in possession of any such remains or objects are required to issue an inventory of any human remains or funerary objects. As of November 16, 1993, agencies must have issued a written summary of all funerary objects not associated with human remains, or sacred or cultural objects under their control, along with all available information on geographical or cultural affiliation of such items. In any case where such items can be associated with specific tribes or groups of tribes, the agency is required to provide notice of the item in question to the tribe or tribes. Upon request, each agency is required to return any such item to any lineal descendant or specific tribe with whom such item is associated. There are various additional requirements imposed upon the Secretary.

Contemporary Native Americans

In seeking answers to questions about Native Americans, remember there are more than 554 Indian tribes and Alaska Native groups within the united states that speak more than 250 languages. Each Indian nation has its own culture, history and identity. Since no two tribes are exactly alike, what is good for one tribe may not be good for another. Consequently, there are no simple solutions to the many challenges facing Indian nations today.

Although only two generations away from the "old way" of life; hunting, fishing, gathering, sowing, etc., American Indians today occupy all professional fields, they are doctors, police, firefighters, foresters and surveyors. Today Indian fathers and mothers work to straddle values between two different worlds, their Indian culture and the current social system of the dominant society. They traverse between the dominant society and their culture as citizens and productive members of both.

Today Indians number approximately 1.2 M, with about 900,000 living on or near Indian reservations. Unemployment on Indian reservations averages about 37%. They experience extreme lack of economic opportunities and a lower than average quality of life when measured against the dominant society. Still the American Indian today proudly maintains an independent cultural identity. American Indians occupy a unique status in this country as it relates to society, political association, cultural identity and relation with the federal government.

Tribal Resources

The following are contact resources for the Native American Reservations and Pueblos mentioned in this book. You may call or write for locations, attractions, and further information pertaining to that specific tribe.

What you may not request is information regarding ghosts, hauntings and the paranormal, for the obvious reason that, this information is not available to the public.

When visiting any Pueblo or Reservation keep in mind that each is a sovereign government. Obey their laws and respect the privacy of the residents.

Ceremonial events which are preformed and timed to the earth's seasons, can take place at a moments notice. Above all when attending such ceremonies behave as you would in a church. Avoid asking personal questions regarding the meanings of ceremonial garb, songs, etc. Remember you are on private property so respect cemeteries, homes, and do not ever climb on kivas, etc.

Always check at the Pueblo/Reservation office before taking movies and photographs, if in doubt, ask the office personnel.

Pascua-Yaqui Tribal Council
7474 S. Camino de Oeste, Tucson, AZ 85746, (602) 883-2838

Colorado River Indian Tribes
Rt. 1, Box 23-B, Parker, AZ 85344, (602) 669-9211

Ak-Chin Indian Community
Rt. 2, Box 27, Maricopa, AZ 85239, (602) 568-2227

White Mountain Apache Tribe
P.O. Box 700, Whiteriver, AZ 85941, (602) 338-4346

Hualapai Tribal Council
P.O. Box 168, Peach Springs, AZ 86434, (602) 769-2216

San Carlos Apache Tribal Council
P.O. Box O, San Carlos, AZ 85550, (602) 475-2361

Tohono O'Odham Tribal Council
P.O. Box 837, Sells, AZ 85634 (602), 383-2221

Hopi Tribal Council
P.O. Box 123, Kyakotsmovi, AZ 86039, (602) 734-2441

All the Pueblos in New Mexico mentioned may be contacted through:
Pueblo Cultural Center
2401 12th Street, NW
Albuquerque, New Mexico 87104 (505) 843-7270
1-800-766-4405 (outside of New Mexico)
http://www.indianpueblo.org/index.shtml#toc

Take Action Resources

My intention on listing the following organizations is to provide you the readers with avenues of recourse by way of information and hopefully motivate you to take personal action. I sincerely believe we all can accomplish a better society, environment and ultimately world through letter writing, donating funds and taking personal responsibility. I encourage you to support 'indigenous' and human rights organizations, environmental causes, and the principles of non-violent social change. Please take the time to contact one or more of these organizations for information, then with one united voice, we all will resolve to make a positive change for our environment, our species and future.

Native American Rights Fund

1506 Broadway, Boulder, CO 80302
(303) 447-8760 www.narf.org/
A national non-profit organization that provides legal representation and technical assistance to tribes, organizations and individuals.

Futures For Children

9600 Tennyson St., N.E., Albuquerque, NM 87122
(800) 545-6843 www.futureofchildren.org/
A nonprofit organization which works to improve the well-being of American Indian children by teaching self-help skills and community development methodologies.

www.indiancircle.com

A web site of various Indian Nations with related links.

U'wa Defense Project

Project Underground at: (510) 705-8982 www.moles.org
An organization who's aim is in preserving Native American culture in Northeastern Colombia from oil companies drilling their traditional lands.

United Farm Workers Union

P.O.Box 62, Keene, CA 93531

(661) 823-6252 www.ufw.org

Historic non-violent union of farm workers dedicated to a safe working environment and restricting pesticide overuse.

Hecel Oyakapi

14431 Ventura Blvd., PMB 255, Sherman Oaks, CA 91423

(818) 788-1482 www.lakotastory.org

A nonprofit organization which is creating a preforming Arts Center to promote the Lakota culture.

Southern Poverty Law Center

P.O. Box 548, Montgomery, AL 36177-9621

www.splcenter.org/

Organization that combats hate, racism, and intolerance throughout the nation.

High Country News

P.O. Box 1090, Paonia, Co 81428

1-800-905-1155 www.hcn.org

A newspaper committed to the preservation of the west.

Direct Relief International

27 So. La Patera Lane, Santa Barbara, CA 93117

www.directrelief.org/

Every single cent of every dollar received is directly used internationally responding to crisises throughout the world.

Doctors without Borders USA

P. O. Box 110, New York, NY 10277-1218

(212) 655-3759 www.dwb.org/

International organization of healthcare workers who donate their time to fighting disease throughout the world. Awarded the 1999 Nobel Peace Prize.

www.all-mart.com/

A wonderful web site listing environmental organizations on the internet.

Amnesty International USA

P.O. Box 96756, Washington, DC 20077-7131
www.amnesty.org/
Organization which advocates the ending of human torture by governments throughout the world through letter writing and distributing information.

Sierra Club

85 Second St., San Francisco, CA 94105-3441
(415) 977-5500 www.sierraclub.org/
Environmental organization whose purpose is to promote the responsible use of the earth's ecosystems and resources.

Human Rights Campaign

919 18th Street, NW, Washington, DC 20006
(202) 628-4160 www.hrcusa.org/
National organization of gay and lesbians that politically advocates for their right to equality.

Forest Guardians

1411 Second St., Santa Fe, NM 87505
(505) 988-9126 www.fguardians.org/
Leads the fight to protect and restore the forests, rivers, grasslands, wildlife of the Southwest.

Green Peace USA

1436 "U" St.- NW, Washington, DC 20009
1-800-326-0959 www.greenpeaceusa.org/
International organization that uses non-violent, creative confrontation to expose global environmental problems to force solutions.

Resource Center for Non-Violence

515 Broadway, Santa Cruz, CA 95060
(831) 423-1626 www.rcnv.org/
Dedicated to promoting the principals of non-violent social change and enhancing the quality of life and human dignity.

www.capecod.net/~ccunning/

A web site dedicated to the furtherance of world peace with many resources.

Foundation for International Community Assistance

1101 14th St., N.W., Washington, DC 20005

(202) 682-1535 www.villagebanking.org

International world bank for the poor which provides small loans, which helps the poor gain the opportunity to create their own jobs—by providing the capital they need.

The following Web sites are hosted by courageous women organizations. These sites are devoted to ending the torture, mental abuse and death directed towards women throughout the world. Please support the work of these heroic human beings.

www.equalitynow.org
www.rawa.org
www.womenforwomen.org
www.htcfl.org

References

Arizona Department of Tourism
Arizona Department of Commerce
Arizona State Parks
Arizona State Archives

IAIA-Institute of American Indian Arts,
Santa Fe, New Mexico
Santa Fe Visitors Guide, 2000
Staff of the Santa Fe Convention and Visitors Bureau
New Mexico Department of Tourism
Pueblo Cultural Center, Albuquerque, New Mexico
Southwestern Indian Tribes, Tom and Mark Bahti,
KC Publications, 1999

Other Books by Antonio R. Garcez

Adobe Angels—Arizona Ghost Stories
Published 1998
ISBN 0-9634029-5-1

Adobe Angels—Ghost Stories of O'Keeffe Country
Published 1998
ISBN 0-9634029-6-X

Adobe Angels—The Ghosts of Las Cruces
and Southern New Mexico
Published 1996
ISBN 0-9634029-4-3

Adobe Angels—The Ghosts of Santa Fe and Taos
Revised 1995
ISBN 0-9634029-3-5

Adobe Angels—The Ghosts of Albuquerque
Published 1992
ISBN 0-9634029-2-7

Future books will include research and travels into the states of California, Utah, Colorado, Nevada and more.

About the Author

photo: The Portrait Place

Antonio R. Garcez graduated with a B.A. from California State University at Northridge, then attended Graduate school at the University of Wisconsin. Antonio resides and continues to write from his home in New Mexico.